# simple flies

# simple
# flies

flies you can tie with three materials or less

(exclusive of hook & thread)

## C. BOYD PFEIFFER

The Countryman Press

Woodstock, Vermont

Copyright © 2005 by C. Boyd Pfeiffer

First Edition

Library of Congress Cataloging-in-Publication Data has been applied for.

ISBN 0-88150-638-9

Book design by Carol Jessop, Black Trout Design
Cover and interior photographs by the author

Published by The Countryman Press, P.O. Box 748, Woodstock, Vermont 05091

Distributed by W. W. Norton & Company, Inc., 500 Fifth Avenue, New York, NY 10110

Printed in China by R. R. Donnelley

10 9 8 7 6 5 4 3 2 1

# CONTENTS

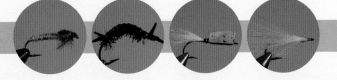

Why tie simple flies? Are they as effective as complex flies?
Offers some tricks of the trade and examples of tiers who
originated and used simple flies.

Illustrates basic tools and materials that can substitute for several in tying a fly. Includes choices of materials and suggestions
for substitutes, with a brief discussion of materials such as
thread, sealers, yarn, chenille, dubbing, floss, hackle (wet and
dry), stranded flash materials, stranded wing materials, tinsels
and wraps, lead wire, furs, hair for wings, body hair, beads and
cones, eyes (all types), and more.

Covers the basics of tying, including tying down, tying off, using
head cement and epoxy, making neatly tapered heads, and
tying in weed guards. Helps avoid problems such as lumpy
bodies, with tips for proper positioning of materials, proper
technique in tying wings and bodies, using thread as a ribbing,
and combining tails and wings in dry flies. Also includes possibilities for making one-material flies, no-body flies, no-tail flies,
no-wing wet and dry flies, using bulky synthetics to build up
body and wings, and coloring thread to make ribbing or heads.

# CONTENTS

# A NOTE TO THE READER

All instructions in this book assume right-handed tiers who work with the jaws of the fly-tying vise pointed to the right and who handle thread bobbins with their right hands. If you are left-handed, then instructions and hand-use directions will have to be reversed. The same applies to the photos; all show a right-handed tier's perspective. Also, many photos have been taken with larger-than-normal materials and thread for the sake of clarity.

Please note that there are references to using lead wire and lead dumbbell eyes. In some areas, lead is prohibited; these materials will therefore have to be eliminated or replaced with non-lead substitutes.

To Brenda
and
To my friends in fly tying and fly fishing—
you know who you are.

# ACKNOWLEDGMENTS

You learn by doing and failing (and sometimes accomplishing something). But the best way to learn is from friends. Fortunately, I have some great friends with whom I have shared ideas, learned tying methods and shortcuts, and tested ideas and theories without being scoffed at too much. Friends such as Lefty Kreh, Ed Russell, Chuck Edghill, Norm Bartlett, Jim Heim, Bill May, Jack Goellner, Joe Zimmer and others have shared their fly-tying skills with me over the years, helping me both develop my own skills and feed my impatience by inventing simple flies. My thanks also to the many writers, fly tiers, friends, casual acquaintances, and fly fishermen who, often without knowing it (and perhaps without my knowing it at the time), helped shape this book by sharing ideas and ideals in fly tying and fly fishing. My thanks also to Kermit Hummel and the staff at Countryman Press for their patience when deadlines got short. My special thanks to my wife, Brenda, who through a very hectic year and a heavy schedule of writing, tying, and shooting photos, always gave me the time to do my thing and grease the writing-project wheels that were squeaking most loudly.

ne of my best friends uses simple flies of his own design. One of his patterns is a surface bug for which he clips a bundle of deer hair, trims it to length, seals the butt ends with hot-melt glue, and then glues the hair close to the rear of a hook shank. He then slots a bottle cork with a hacksaw and hot-glues that to the hook also. The process is not fly tying but fly gluing, and the result is a surface bug that has only two materials, no paint, no thread, and no class—but it catches a lot of fish.

It is a good basic cork popper, though not one that you will see in stores or that any fly tier would admit to "tying." But it works. The fly's originator, Capt. Norm Bartlett, has about seven IGFA records (not all on this fly, though) and continues to catch more than his share of fish on his personal fishing trips. Norm does just as well for his clients, whether he's finding fish for them on the Chesapeake Bay or on fresh waters throughout the mid-Atlantic area.

Other tiers go to the other extreme. Bob Meade ties flies that are as different from a basic Mickey Finn or Humpy as museum-quality waterfowl carvings and art are from battered working decoys thrown out on a windswept marsh. Bob's flies have hooks, but otherwise look like wasps, bees, and even anatomically correct female praying mantis. His flies are for serious collectors and aficionados of the art. They "live" under glass domes, never to see the water, never to be spotted by a hungry fish. English tier Phil Willock ties flies that so closely replicate live insects that examples sent to this country were confiscated by U.S. Customs agents who mistook them for real insects. Yas Yamashita has similar skills, as do a handful of other tiers. Some tie

and frame classic feather-wing salmon flies. These are flies of the past, often made on blind-eye hooks with snells or gut loops. But most of these tiers will also admit that the best flies are often the simple, fuzzy, suggestive ones, and not the precise imitations of real fish food.

The late Poul Jorgensen, who tied exquisitely precise nymph patterns, was the first to admit that very simple, suggestive patterns will work best. Just why they do is a matter of conjecture. One theory is that precisely tied patterns have little movement in the water because they lack soft materials that can wave around and invite close inspection by a fish. Many precise imitations are trout patterns, and trout, in the clean waters where they live, can immediately tell the difference between a real *Ephemera guttulata* and a carefully assembled collection of materials designed to replicate a green drake nymph.

Couple this with the fact that a simple, suggestive fly invites immediate gobbling by a fish whose table manners are atrocious. In its eat-or-be-eaten, kill-or-be-killed, grab-it-or-lose-it world, a fish learns to grab anything going by in the current or floating nearby, knowing that it can blow the food out of its mouth should the morsel prove to be less than tasty. Were we to do this, we would be banned from the table, even in a fast-food restaurant.

Without intending any disrespect to those expert and patient tiers of collectibles or the more complex fishing patterns, many fly fishers understand that simple flies have a lot of advantages. The idea of simple, quick, and easy patterns is not new, although it has not been the subject of an entire book, or even many book chapters and magazine articles. But simple patterns have been published now and again.

Edward Ringwood Hewitt, the famous trout fisherman and author of the 1920s, described making lightweight, simple flies that had only tails and large hackles. You can't get a much simpler dry fly. Hewitt went even further with his Neversink Skater. This is nothing more than a hugely oversize hackle on a hook, with no tail, body, wings, or other materials. It was designed, according to Hewitt's writings, to simulate butterflies that trout often lunged after when these beautiful insects danced in the air close to the water's surface.

The same approach can be used with any type of fly for any kind of fly fishing. In addition to Norm Bartlett's no-tie cork bug or the hackle flies of Hewitt, you can find my Simple One saltwater fly from 40 years ago, single-material Glo Bugs for steelhead, simple streamers for trout, one-material flies for trout and smallmouths, my two-material hellgrammite pattern for smallmouths, my one-material fly-fisher's equivalent of a plastic purple worm, basic 'cuda flies, simple bonefish patterns, basic crabs, and simple crayfish. You can also find many flies tied with no more than three materials for panfish, shad, pike, Pacific salmon, saltwater game, spring-creek trout, and just about every other kind of fish.

Too often, flies are made more complex than required. The extreme examples are the traditional Atlantic salmon flies that have become works of art, museum pieces, and collectibles. While many of us admire the flies' beauty and the creativity and skill required to make them, simple hair-wing salmon flies based on the same designs work just as well. While fishing the Grande Cascapedia in the fall of 2003, a friend and I found that the best pattern was a simple, black marabou leech fished deep. It outfished by a wide margin standard (and much prettier) hair-wing patterns that have been around for decades.

Many fly patterns include minute details even though the basic design is only a suggestion of the actual bait or insect that it is copying. By ignoring the small details that fish will undoubtedly also ignore, we can tie simple flies that are quicker to make and are just as effective as more complex patterns.

This book includes tying steps for simple flies as a way of showing examples of flies that will take fish anywhere. It does not try to show all the possibilities of simple flies. A simple two- or three-material dry-fly design could father hundreds of "patterns," depending upon the types and colors of feathers and body materials used. Similarly, simple saltwater streamers can be tied with a vast variety of materials and colors. This book is designed to show you a variety of ways in which you can tie simple, easy flies, reduce standard patterns to their elements to create original flies that are often just as effective as standard patterns, and suggest ways in which you can reduce various steps to simplify a fly that would otherwise take more time, materials, and tying steps. It is also designed to stimulate your imagination so that you can extend the theories, concepts, and patterns to your own tying, whether you need trout flies, saltwater streamers, tropical flats patterns, or warmwater flies and bugs. I hope this book will help you reduce flies to the basics, to their simplest forms and functions. Believe me, the fish won't care.

The premise behind this project was to create a tying book that would include patterns and methods requiring no more than three materials, exclusive of the hook and tying thread. (Originally, my thought was for a book about flies with no more than one or two materials, but that proved to be a little too restrictive.) It evolved into a book of flies that are reduced not only in materials, but also in complexity. For example, some spun or stacked hair patterns (such as a Messinger Bucktail Frog) might include only two or three materials, and thus qualify under the "three materials or fewer" category. Other examples might include a mouse with a deer-hair body, cord tail, and suede ears, or a Henshall-style hair bug with bucktail legs and wings and a banded deer-hair body. All of these use only a few materials, but most tiers would not put any of them in the "quick and easy" category. Spinning and stacking deer hair is a skill learned over time. Even with this skill perfected, spinning and stacking a bug body takes some time to do properly. Accordingly, I have not included anything that involves spinning or stacking deer hair.

The same thought applies to carefully shaped and painted cork and balsa bugs. Such bugs might consist of only tails and cork bodies, but painting a body and adding eyes can add a lot of work and require a lot of time. Cork and balsa bugs can be extremely simple—like Capt. Norm Bartlett's glue-gun bug—but they can also entail shaping, sanding, gluing, priming, and painting a body, and then tying materials to the hook. With complex bugs, the answer is an assembly-line process that will allow you to make a lot of them at once, following one step in the process at a time, rather than going through a series of different steps to make each bug.

If you want slightly fancier flies than those shown in this book, you can gussy up many simple patterns with additions and variations. For example, you can tie a simple, suggestive trout nymph with nothing more than a body of EZ-Dub, yarn, chenille, Ultra Chenille, or dubbing, and a head of peacock herl. But by adding a wing case, or a tail, or gills, or a hackle, you can have a wide range of new designs, none of which requires more than three materials. They can be tied in different sizes and colors, adding to the rich possibilities for fly tiers to customize simple techniques for their particular purposes. You can make a simple streamer consisting of a body and wing (synthetic or natural), but then color the wing or body with a felt-tip pen, add a tail or throat, make a two-layer wing, add some flash material to the wing, or make a two-part body. Do any of these and you have created a whole new range of uncomplicated streamer designs. The possibilities are endless.

Add the combinations of colors possible in just those two examples, and you have hundreds of flies that can be tied simply, easily, and with little time at the bench. The result is more time fishing, and more flies in more boxes to give you more choices to throw at any fish. Ultimately, that is what fly tying is all about. The purpose of fly tying is to tie flies, and the purpose of having flies that you have tied is to fish.

chapter

## TOOLS

You will need a modicum of tools and materials for fly tying. Gone are the days when fly tiers tied by hand without a vise, or when simple pin vises represented the technological cutting edge. In addition to a vise, there are other basic tools that you will need to become proficient.

**Vise.** There are dozens of fly-tying vises on the market, ranging from very inexpensive styles to those that cost hundreds of dollars. Those that come in kits are typically pretty poor. For best results, get a vise such as one of the bare-bones but excellent Griffin models, or opt for a better Griffin, Dyna-King, Abel, Regal, or similar vise. Just realize that you don't need to spend a lot of bucks to get a good vise. A basic Griffin will sell for around $40.

You have a choice of several styles. Rotary styles are best for those who tie great numbers of flies (commercial tiers, for instance) or for tiers who make flies on which a lot of materials are wrapped around the hook shank. A rotary vise is helpful because it does allow inspecting the fly from the far side by rotating the jaws. Other vises also allow this without being true in-line rotary.

Vises come in both clamp-on and pedestal styles, with the clamp-on best if you are working at a basic fly-tying bench. The clamp provides rock-solid support for the vise. A pedestal style with a heavy base can be used on any table and will not mar the surface or underside of the table top as a clamp-on vise might, but a pedestal vise does not allow the vertical adjustment possible with a clamp-on. That stated, I prefer a pedestal style that I can move around, adjust as desired, and take with me on trips.

Most vises have jaws that will take a wide range of hooks, although some vises (such as those from HMH) have removable jaws that allow using fine jaws for tiny flies and large jaws for salt- and warmwater patterns. Jaws are tightened by a lever that when pulled back and down operates a cam to tighten the jaw against a collet, or by a lever-action thumbscrew that tightens the jaws on the hook. Both designs work fine.

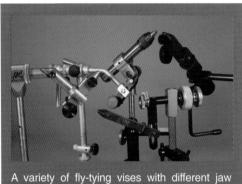

A variety of fly-tying vises with different jaw designs, pedestal or clamp mounts, and other features are available for your particular needs.

**Light.** You will need a good light for tying. There are special fly-tying lamps, including models that sit on your tying desk, clamp onto the vise post, stand on the floor, have magnifiers, or have bulbs balanced for natural light of 5500 Kelvin temperature so that materials appear as they do in daylight. All of these are good, but you can get along quite nicely with a small student's desk lamp taking a standard bulb (usually 60 watt) or one of the small halogen or high-intensity table lamps. These are relatively inexpensive. Just make sure that your lamp sits with the light high enough to clear the vise while providing enough room to wrap materials without hitting the light.

Get at least two pairs of scissors—one with fine, short blades for delicate cutting and one with heavier, longer, coarse blades for cutting heavy materials. Serrated blades—or one serrated and one smooth—make it easier to cut materials such as synthetics that would otherwise slip.

Be sure to buy fly-tying scissors with holes that comfortably fit your fingers.

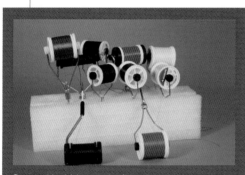

Several bobbins make it easy to store and use several different threads of different sizes and/or colors. For best results, purchase only ceramic-tip bobbins.

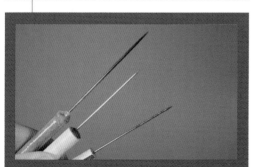

You can make or buy bodkins, which are basically needles mounted in handles. Bodkins are used for depositing head cement or freeing materials that you have inadvertently bound down with the thread.

**Scissors.** Get good scissors, preferably two pairs. Buy one very fine pair of scissors to cut thread, trim hackle, and cut fine, delicate materials. Get a larger pair of coarse scissors for cutting lead wire, metal tinsel and wire, coarse materials, and so forth. Serrated edges are best to prevent materials from slipping while cutting.

Be sure to buy fly-tying scissors with holes that comfortably fit your fingers.

**Bobbins.** A bobbin lets you tie without handling the thread with your fingers. Most bobbins used to be made with brass tubes and simple brackets to hold the thread spool, and some are still made this way, but don't even bother with these. Buy a bobbin with a ceramic tip (a ring in the end of the tube). This type will not fray your thread and will never wear out. If you tie a lot of large flies or bugs, get a bobbin with a long tube; the long tube is necessary for clearing the bodies of bugs and large flies as you wrap around them. For most fly tying, you will do fine with a short-tube bobbin. If you work with a lot of different sizes and colors of thread, you might want several bobbins, though you can of course remove and replace thread spools in a single bobbin as needed. I like to have a half-dozen available with different threads.

**Bodkin.** A bodkin (a needle in a handle) is great for working out hackle that has been accidentally bound down with thread, applying a tiny drop of head cement, fraying out body material, and many other tasks. You can buy bodkins wherever fly-tying supplies are sold, but you also can make one by inserting a large needle, eye first, into a 4-inch length of wood dowel (drill a tiny hole and glue the needle in place). Keep several of different sizes for a variety of tying purposes.

**Hackle pliers.** These are a must for wrapping hackle around a hook shank, and they're also useful for holding and wrapping other materials. You have a choice of several styles—the flat spring-type English style, the wire- or rod-type of English style, and the rotary style. This last has small gripping jaws attached to a hinged joint and a handle. You can grip materials and wrap around a hook shank without repositioning the pliers as required with other styles. Repositioning is required with standard hackle pliers to prevent twisting the material or hackle with each full rotation.

The above tools are the basics and probably all you need for most simple flies, but you probably will be glad to have the following tools as well.

**Comb.** Any small comb can be used to comb out the underfur from animal skins. You can use the underfur for dubbing or discard it when you want to make wings and throats from the guard hairs. Small moustache combs and eyelash combs from drug or cosmetic stores are ideal for this.

**Dubbing teaser.** Dubbing teasers are rough, so that they fray out materials to make them shaggy and buggy looking. Many are commercially available. You can make one from the hook side of a hook-and-loop fastener (such as Velcro). Glue the piece of hook-and-loop material to a tongue depressor or craft stick.

**Half-hitch tool.** These small, tapered tools with a hole in one end are ideal for making half hitches to finish a wrap on a fly's head. Use the tool by looping the thread around it, then placing the hole over the hook eye and pulling the thread to slide the loop off the tool and onto the head of the fly. A half-hitch tool with a deep hole (so you can slide it over the hook shank) can be used to secure materials with a locking half hitch as you tie.

**Whip finisher.** You can use your fingers to make a whip finish on any fly (I do), but there are tools that also accomplish this. These are available in two styles; the Matarelli lets you make a whip finish on any part of a fly, while other brands allow a whip finish only at the head of the fly. With your fingers, you can make any number of whip-finish wraps on any part of the fly.

**Tool rack.** Most of these are made of wood, foam, or plastic and include a variety of round and square holes of different sizes to hold everything from bodkins to head cement bottles, scissors to whip finishers. They keep tools from spreading all over the bench.

**Bobbin threaders.** These simple tools, mostly wire or mono loops, make pulling the thread through a bobbin's tube much easier.

**Bobbin cleaner.** Bobbins ultimately get clogged with wax from threads. These cleaners are mostly thin rods or short lengths of thick mono used to push wax out of a bobbin tube. You can make your own from a short length of thick mono from a lawn trimmer.

**Material dispensers.** These come in a wide range of types and styles, depending upon the materials and the manufacturer. They include plastic compartment boxes with holes in the bottom through which stored dubbing can be pulled; small bottles, bins,

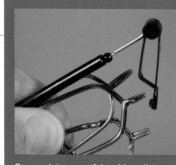

Several types of hackle pliers are available. These tools are useful not only for winding hackle, but also for working with other materials that are wound on the hook shank. Ideal are the relatively new rotating hackle pliers that prevent materials from twisting as you wrap them in place.

Small combs such as those for cosmetic use are ideal for combing out underfur when preparing fur for wing material and for getting underfur to use as dubbing.

Dubbing teasers are available commercially, or you can make your own from a Popsicle stick and the hook side of a hook-and-loop fastener (such as Velcro). These are ideal for making a fly shaggy and buggy looking.

Half-hitch tools are ideal for making locking wraps on a fly to hold materials.

Using a half-hitch tool requires making a loop of thread around the tapered end of the tool and then positioning it on the eye of the hook. Because hook sizes and eyes vary so much, several sizes of half-hitch tools are necessary if you tie a wide variety of flies.

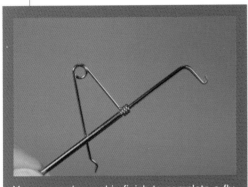

You can make a whip finish to complete a fly with your fingers, or you can use a tool like this to achieve the wraps around the fly's

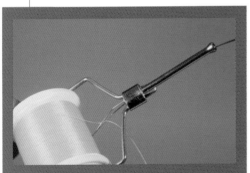

You can buy a bobbin threader or make one with a doubled piece of fine wire or monofilament. This simple, handy tool lets you pull the thread through the tube of a bobbin.

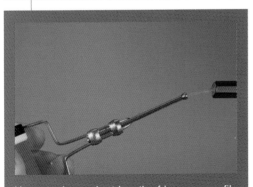

Use a tool or a short length of heavy monofilament to clean built-up wax out of the bobbin tube.

and round plastic containers for beads; spool containers (such as those from Spirit River) for stranded materials such as chenille and yarn; long pill-like containers for hooks and beads; racks and tubes for flash material; and so on.

Just remember that the basics of fly tying are a simple but sturdy vise, a good light source, a bobbin or two to hold thread, two pairs of scissors (one fine/delicate, one sturdy/coarse), hackle pliers, and a bodkin. The rest of tools you can add as desired when you need them for particular patterns or tying techniques.

## MATERIALS

**Hooks.** Hooks for fly tying come in hundreds of different styles from a dozen or more companies. Add to that the different lengths, wire weights, finishes, and sizes, and you have thousands of choices. The basics of fly-hook design revolve around the bend of the hook. Some are completely symmetrical (Perfect bend); others have a squared-off bend (Sneck); some have an almost round bend (Aberdeen); others have a sharper kink at the lower part of the bend (Limerick, O'Shaughnessy, Sproat); some have special shank configurations for salmon fishing (Dublin, Wilson, York); and still others have very curved shanks for making shrimp, scud, and nymph patterns.

Many hooks are available not only in regular lengths but also longer and shorter shank lengths. These are usually indicated by an X system, with 1X-short indicating a hook that has a shank length of the next smaller standard-length hook and 1X-long indicating a hook with a shank length of the next larger standard hook. Hook shanks range from about 3X-short to 10X-long.

A similar X system is used to describe hooks that are made of finer or stouter wire than normal. A hook 2X finer for dry-fly fishing would have the wire of a standard hook two sizes smaller, while a 2X-stout hook would be made of wire normally used for a hook two sizes larger.

Hook manufacturers and experts argue whether the X scale is based on the next available size or the next hypothetical size, even though it is not made. Thus, you can meet those who argue that a 1X-short size 12 hook has a shank length equivalent to that of a size 14 hook, and others who claim that it has a shank as long as that of a size 13 hook, which is technically a size whether or not it is made. Similarly, you can start arguments over whether a 3X-long size 6 hook has the shank length of a size 3 (not made) or a size 1 (the third size up that is manufactured). The bottom line is that any hook that is "X-rated" fine or stout is made of lighter or heavier wire than the "normal" hook, while anything that is "X-rated" longer or shorter has a longer or shorter shank than that designed for the "normal" hook. The higher the number, the greater the fineness, stoutness, length, or shortness.

This affects how you tie and what you tie, and can also affect materials—and the number of materials—that you use to make simple flies. For example, you can use a heavy-wire hook that will help sink a nymph and perhaps obviate having to add weight with small dumbbell eyes, a cone head, a bead, or wire. Similarly, a light-wire hook for a dry fly might lessen the need for shaggy dubbing or a dense hackle to help float the fly. Long and short shanks are primarily made to permit designing imitations that are similar in shape and profile to the naturals. Long-shank hooks are a must for tying minnow and baitfish imitations, while a short-shank hook comes closest to the shape of a freshwater scud.

There are so many hooks and hook styles today that they are seldom named any more. Often they are known by numbers. As a result, fly tiers and some fly fishers often talk of using a 34011 (long-shank stainless-steel Mustad hook), 34007 (regular-shank stainless-steel Mustad hook), C12U (Gamakatsu caddisfly hook), CS15 (Partridge extra-long streamer hook), 135 (Dai-Riki scud/shrimp hook), X510 (Daiichi short-shank salmon-fly hook), 33903 (Mustad popper-body hook) or 947BL (Tiemco swimming-nymph hook). There are hundreds like these from which to choose.

Those interested in knowing more details about hooks or having a ready reference for most of the hooks available can check out *Hooks for the Fly*, by William E. Schmidt (Stackpole Books, Mechanicsburg, PA).

**Thread.** Thread is essential to fly tying. As with hooks, there are a multitude of choices with fly-tying threads. At one time, silk thread was the standard, but today there are many good nylon and polyester threads in a great variety of sizes, styles, and colors. Thread comes in sizes from about 15/0 (the lightest) to 3/0 (the heaviest). You can get even heavier threads—such as sizes A, D, E, and EE—but most of them are better suited to rod building and jig tying than to most fly tying.

Thread comes in a wide variety of sizes and colors for almost any conceivable use in fly tying.

**Thread sealers.** Thread sealer, sometimes called head cement, is used to coat, penetrate, and seal the thread wrap at the head of a fly to protect it, keep the whip finish from unraveling, and sometimes to provide a base on which you can paint eyes. These products are available in environmentally friendly styles (such as those from Loon Outdoors) as well as solvent-based formulas. Many fly tiers use Sally Hansen Hard as Nails fingernail polish, since it is easy to get and use. The best sealers are usually high-solvent types that penetrate into the head of the fly, although this kind of sealer requires repeated coats to build up the head. A head cement that's too thick will float on top of the fly's head; this makes for a one-coat application, but will not penetrate well.

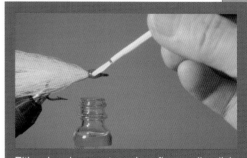
Either head cement or clear fingernail polish can be used to seal the heads of flies. You can use the brush that comes with fingernail polish or a bodkin to deposit a tiny drop of cement.

Hackle can be bought in strung bundles, on necks or half-necks, on saddles or half-saddles, or loose. These important feathers come in natural and dyed colors and in a wide range of sizes.

Bend a hackle to see the webbing and determine whether the feather is better for wet flies or dry flies. Stiff, shiny fibers and very little web indicate a dry-fly hackle; soft fibers and a lot of web make a feather better for sinking flies.

Yarn is a basic body material that can be used on a lot of flies. It is available in a wide range of colors, materials, textures, and sizes in fly shops, craft stores, and fabric stores.

Chenille is also available in many colors and sizes for tying many types of wet flies, streamers, saltwater flies, and terrestrials.

An easy way to seal the heads of larger flies is to use standard two-part clear epoxy. This material typically becomes too difficult to control on flies smaller than about size 6, but this depends upon your skill and the type of fly. If you use epoxy, tie a bunch of flies and then add the finish to all of them at once. If you tie only a dozen or so, you can use five-minute epoxy. If you're working with a larger number of flies, get epoxy with a longer working life (usually about 30 minutes). Once the fly's head is coated with epoxy, place the fly on a rotator tool so that the coating will not sag or drip. See chapter 2, "Simple Tying Steps, Tricks, and Tips," for more details on application.

**Hackle.** Hackle is widely available through fly shops and mail-order catalogs. Basically, the term refers to the feathers from the neck of a bird, most often a chicken, although hackles from grouse, wood ducks, pheasants, and other birds are used for tying. Dry-fly hackle has stiff, shiny fibers with little "web" (the fuzzy, softer portion of the feather along the quill), since any web will soak up moisture and make the fly sink rapidly or not float well. Wet-fly hackle has a lot of webby fibers, since the desire here is to have a fly that sinks. To check for the "webbiness" of hackle, hold a single feather up to the light to see the amount of webbing between the individual fibers. Popular today are those soft-hackle flies that have longer than normal (at least longer than in the past) hackle fibers to make for a very buggy fly with a lot of action and movement in the water.

You can buy hackle by the neck or by the half-neck, as well as in packets of individual feathers. Long "saddle" hackles are available on the skin or in strung bunches of a given size that are good for a multitude of flies. Chicken hackle comes in a wide range of colors and patterns. Although most of the patterns are natural, the colors can be either natural or dyed. For instance, you can get a natural grizzly hackle (mottled gray, black, and white) or one which has been dyed.

**Yarn.** This material works well for simple bodies. It comes in both synthetic and natural materials, with synthetics usually the least expensive and best. It is also available in a multitude of thicknesses and colors, variegated colors, and various textures.

**Chenille.** Chenille comes in fine grades such as Ultra Chenille and Vernille, and in standard types that are suitable for most tying. You can also get chenilles that are variegated, along with the plastic chenilles (such as Ice Chenille and Estaz) that are very sparkly. Chenille comes in many sizes.

**Floss.** Floss is made of very fine strands of materials, either silk or synthetic, and is used to make shiny, smooth bodies on flies such as a Royal Coachman. Like other materials, it is available in many sizes and colors.

**Dubbing substitutes.** Standard dubbing is time consuming to make and use. It requires cutting and mixing furs and/or synthetics, then waxing the thread (so the material will stick to the thread) or forming a thread loop in which to twist the dubbing before wrapping it around the hook shank. Fortunately, tiers who favor simple flies can also get stranded dubbing materials such as Gudebrod EZ-Dub, E-Zee Bug, mohair, and others, which have a ragged, buggy appearance in very lifelike colors, yet are as easy as yarn to tie onto a hook.

Synthetic dubbings that are stranded (like yarn) make it easy to get a dubbed look by simply wrapping a material around a hook.

**Flash materials.** By adding flash materials such as Flashabou, Krystal Flash, Super G Flash, and others to the wing of a streamer fly, you can greatly increase its fish-catching ability.

**Wire, tinsels, and such.** Metal and plastic (often Mylar) tinsels are available in many colors and sizes for making shiny bodies. Wire in various sizes and non-tarnishing colors is becoming increasingly important in fly tying. Braided tinsel-like materials such as Gudebrod HT Braid, Gudebrod Electra Metallic Hologram Braid, and Kreinik braids make it easy to build a minnow-like body on any fly.

Flash materials are easy to add to any streamer or saltwater fly to make it more attractive to fish. Many colors and styles are available.

**Lead (and lead-free) wire.** Wire for weighting hooks is available in lead and lead-free versions in a half dozen sizes. In some areas, lead is not allowed for fishing (this prohibition includes brass, which has trace amounts of lead). In these places, you must use lead-free products, including the weighting wire in your flies.

**Furs and hairs.** Natural furs are taking a back seat to the many synthetics available today. Some furs, however, are irreplaceable. Rabbit fur is used for Zonkers and some chum flies, and body hair from deer, elk, moose, and caribou is popular for making the spun and stacked bugs that are beyond the scope of this book. Bucktail is still a popular material for wings and tails, as is calf tail for wings on smaller flies.

Metal, glass, and plastic beads are being used more and more to tie simple flies—mostly nymphs—and to help weight flies or give them an added bit of color.

**Beads and cone heads.** Relatively new on the fly-fishing scene are the beads and cone heads used to add both color and weight to a fly. They are added to barbless hooks or those with the barbs bent down. It is best to use a hook that has a round bend, so that you don't hit any sharp bends that might prevent the bead from sliding on. Plastic or glass beads are used mostly to add color, with the plastic being lighter than glass. Beads and cone heads made of everything from base metals to tungsten are used to add weight. They also add color and flash with their varied finishes such as gold, brass, copper, black, and nickel. Metal beads and cones simplify adding both weight and flash or color to a fly.

**Tie-on eyes.** Dumbbell eyes made of lead or other metals are used to tie flies such as the Clouser Minnow and other weighted patterns. Dumbbells are best when you want to tie a fly that will ride hook up. Use a hook with a turned-down eye and tie the eye on the top of the hook shank (on the side opposite the bend and point, that is).

**Marabou.** The very soft, fluffy feathers of the African marabou stork have been replaced by similar plumage from turkeys or sometimes chickens (for smaller flies). Marabou is a great material available in many colors and even with barred or mottled patterns. It has an action that is irresistible to most fish.

**Peacock herl.** Add some peacock herl to the head of a fly tied with EZ-Dub, and you have a simple, two-material fly that is easy to tie and a great imitation of a caddis nymph. Thanks to its unique iridescent sheen, peacock is great for caddis heads, toppings for streamers, ribs on fly bodies, and other uses.

Body tubing makes it easy to make simple minnow imitations. Several brands, colors, and sizes are available.

**Rubber or silicone legs.** Thread a few rubber or silicone legs through the foam, cork, or balsa body of a bug and you automatically add some action and make the bug better. You can also add these materials to underwater flies for more action. Legs come in several materials (rubber, silicone, and Lycra) and in solid, variegated, and banded colors.

**Body tubing.** Tubing such as E-Z Body or Corsair is easy to use to make fly and bug bodies that have an iridescent and translucent look that can rival a real minnow's appearance. Chapter 2 shows some neat ways to simplify your tying with these materials.

Colored sheet or cylinder foam lets you make simple bugs for everything from panfish to giant saltwater stripers.

**Foam.** You can buy foam cylinders, formed foam bodies, and sheet foam. All come in a dozen or more colors and in many sizes. The foam bodies and cylinders come in sizes ranging from about ⅛ inch to about ¾ inch. Sheet foam is available in sizes from about 0.5 mm to about 6 mm or ¼ inch. Pre-shaped and formed bodies for making trout terrestrials are also available.

**Cork and balsa bodies.** Cork and occasionally balsa are available in preshaped body forms. Small bottle corks also make good bug bodies. To make simple bugs without cutting, shaping, and sanding the material, use bottle corks that can be glued and tied as poppers, or use bullet-shaped foam, cork, and balsa bodies that work as either sliders or poppers. They are available from small to large sizes for everything from trout and panfish to saltwater and billfish.

**Paints.** I am not in favor of paints, at least when tying simple flies. Paints add several steps to making any bug, since you might have to first fill pits (in cork), then coat the body with a primer, then add two coats of the finish. If you do decide to use paints, it is best to get the all-purpose enamels or the specialty paints such as the "soft" paints from Rainy Riding for painting foam bugs. Normal paints will chip off such bugs any time they are compressed.

2
chapter

# SIMPLE TYING STEPS, TIPS, AND TRICKS

There are a lot of ways to tie simple flies or make standard flies into simpler versions that still attract and catch fish. The basic thinking behind simple fly tying is to reduce a fly to the basic elements that will catch fish. In some cases, this is not easy. Examples that come to mind are the often complex tying steps and many materials used in hellgrammite imitations, stonefly and mayfly nymph imitations, some crayfish patterns, some drys, and some streamers. With some flies, particularly nymph and hellgrammite patterns, it might be difficult to decide exactly which parts make a fish take a fly. Is it the basic shape, size, or color alone? These are basic elements in any fly. Showing fish a fly that's the wrong size might be the equivalent of our seeing a giant potato chip the size of a salad plate or a strip steak the size of a chocolate chip cookie. We might not be too interested in eating, considering the odd, "wrong" size of the food. The wrong color might be the equivalent of our being offered black ice cream or green eggs (with apologies to Dr. Suess). An incorrectly shaped fly might be like our being served lasagna in an ice-cream cone or a lamb chop ground and shaped like a hot dog. All this might be perfectly good and tasty food, but most of us would reject it because it just doesn't look right. Fish react to their food the same way.

In the cases of some nymphs, you might consider how to eliminate materials and tying steps while keeping a pattern the right color, shape, and size. A complicated nymph, for example, can consist of a tail or tails, gills, wing cases, abdomen, rib, thorax, head, legs, and antennae. Perhaps you can reduce such a fly to a shaggy, three-material pattern that suggests a certain shape and color scheme that fish will eat. Some dry flies can be tied with thread bodies, reducing both the number of materials required and the number of tying steps. Naturally, tying a dry fly this way requires that you use the right color of thread; you can't make a thread-bodied Light Cahill with black thread. Using thread for the body also means that you have to want a fly with a thin body.

Often, starting from scratch to design a simple fly works better than trying to simplify a complex pattern that you saw in a book. You can often use a complex fly as a model, maintaining the pattern's general shape and most important feature in your own very simple design.

As noted earlier, simple fly tying requires not only few materials, but also few steps. Were we to use only the tying thread to make a fly with a fat body, we would have to wrap many layers up and down the hook shank to taper the body. This would require as much time—perhaps more—than tying in a proper body material, working the thread forward, and then wrapping the material to complete the body.

The purpose of simple tying is to develop basic flies that are easy to tie with limited materials. The goal is not a ridiculous reduction of materials that results in a poor design or poor fly. Neither is it an attempt to develop flies that are very simple in number of materials, but very complex in tying steps, such as weaving bodies for nymphs or stacking a hair-bodied bass bug.

There are ways by which a lot of flies can be made simpler both by material reduction and easy tying methods. The following tricks will save time and materials at the vise.

**Tying on.** Attach the thread at the point where you will start to add materials. On most wet flies and nymphs, and some streamers, you would start at the rear of the hook shank, right at the bend. This allows you to clip the excess thread, tie on the body and/or tail, then wrap the thread forward to be followed by the body material. A variation of this is tying a tailed fly on which you will eliminate body material and use thread. For this, hold the tail in place on the hook shank and wrap the thread around both the tail and the hook wire; then, after three turns, clip off the excess thread. In essence, you are tying the thread onto the hook while at the same time tying down the tail materials. Make one more turn to cover the clipped tag end of thread and then reverse the thread to evenly cover the hook shank with the thread as a substitute body.

To save time when tying dry flies, attach the thread about one-fourth of the shank length behind the hook eye, and then tie in the upright wing bundle facing forward. You can leave material facing forward (for now) or raise it up with a dam of thread in front of the wings, followed by a smooth, even wrap of thread to the rear of the hook shank, tying in the tail as you work rearward. Then reverse the thread direction and wrap forward neatly to form a tapered body before tying in and winding the hackle.

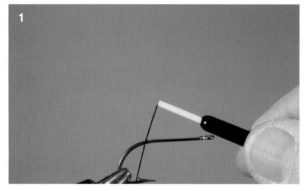

Tying on begins by holding the thread at an angle over the hook shank where you want to attach it.

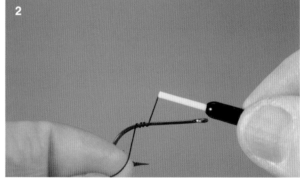

Continue tying on by making a few wraps of the thread around the hook shank as shown here.

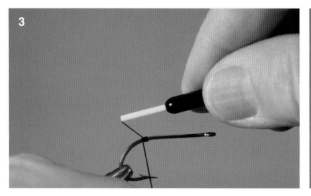

Secure the thread by then wrapping over the previous wraps to "lock" the thread in place on the hook.

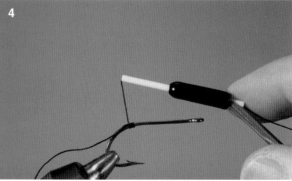

You can clip the long tag end, or you can leave a very long tag end to use later as a rib around the body of the fly.

**Tying off.** You can use a whip-finish tool to complete the head of a fly, but I always prefer using my fingers. I always have them with me, and I don't have to pick up and later put down any tool. Whip-finishing by hand is easy (see the photos), requiring only a series of wraps around the standing part of the thread and the head of the fly, and then pulling the loop tight to secure it. One tip is to hold the standing thread in your left hand using the last two fingers of your hand. Then use the first two fingers and your thumb to pull back any materials, such as a hackle collar or palmered hackle. In addition, it also helps to place your left thumbnail right against the rear edge of the head of the fly, or at the rearmost point where you want the whip finish. Your thumbnail serves as a guide so that you have several wraps in succession in the same general area, and it prevents making a wrap back on the body. This trick is particularly helpful on small flies, though I use it in most of my tying as a quick and easy guide to thread placement.

The best way to finish a fly is to use a whip finish. To do this by hand, hold two fingers over the working thread as shown, and then rotate your fingers while moving the thread to create a loop.

Here, the loop has been created with the rotated fingers.

Wrap the loop of thread over the hook shank (head of the fly) and also the working thread that is now parallel to the hook shank.

Continue making several more wraps around the hook shank and the working thread.

Finish the fly by pulling the working thread to tighten the loop against the head. You can use your fingers for this.

An alternative and better way to tighten a whip finish is to use a bodkin so that you can pull the loop tight without having it twist and knot.

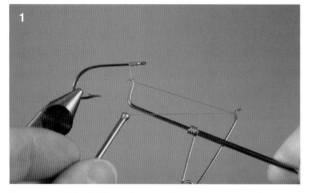

To use a whip-finish tool, pass the working thread around the prongs to make a loop that can be wrapped around the head of the fly. This is shown on a bare hook for clarity.

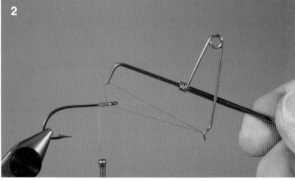

Here, the whip-finish tool is being used to wrap the loop around the fly's head.

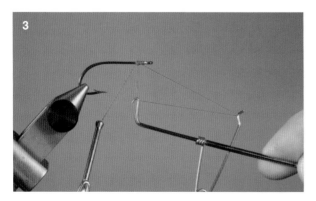

Continue wrapping this way to make several loops or wraps of thread around the head of the fly. Remove the thread from the rear hook on the tool and tighten the loop.

**Using head cement.** The slow way to add head cement to flies is to apply it after tying each fly. You have to finish the fly, clip the thread, open the head-cement bottle, apply the head cement, hang up the fly, and then close the bottle. That's assuming a lid with a built-in brush or applicator. If the lid of your head-cement bottle doesn't have a built-in bodkin or brush, you have to pick up and use an additional tool.

The best solution is to tie a bunch of flies, preferably of one type and size. Then open and use the head cement or fingernail polish, adding the head cement to each fly and hanging the flies on a rack or dryer. This works best for up to a couple dozen flies at a time.

To cement the head of a large fly, I like the standard brush that comes in a Sally Hansen Hard as Nails bottle of nail polish. But I also keep a few other bottles around, using one with a clipped, tapered, pointed brush for smaller flies, and one in which the brush has been replaced with a glued-in needle (to make a bodkin) for very small flies. Thus, I can pick and choose the applicator I need.

Add head cement or epoxy to the head of a fly to seal it, using a bodkin or a small, tapered brush like that in a bottle of fingernail polish.

**Using epoxy.** Epoxy is best as a coating or sealer on large flies. By this, I mean any fly which has a large head. It is important to note that at this writing, all of the available epoxies turn slightly yellow in time. If you are concerned about the head of a fly turning a light wheat to amber color, tie up only enough flies to use for a season, or if you are tying up a larger bunch of flies, coat with epoxy only those that you will use over several months. You can tie flies and keep them in a closed box for years, and then seal them with epoxy as required.

Any of the hobby or craft epoxies will work well. To use epoxy, spread equal amounts of the two parts onto a clean surface. This can be anything: metal, plastic, glass, or stiff paper. Whip or mix thoroughly with a stirrer (stiff coffee stirrers work well) until you have a unified mix. You can tell this state when you no longer see swirls of the two parts showing in the clear mix. Make sure that you scrape up all the epoxy from the mixing surface and around the edges to get a complete mix. At this point, with the flies lined up to be coated, use the coffee stirrer, a bodkin, or a small disposable brush (those from Flex Coat are inexpensive and ideal for large flies) to coat the head or any other part of the fly. Then place the fly on a rotator. These are simple devices that turn at low speed (many fly tiers use low-rpm rotisserie motors) and are fitted with foam circles or drums into which you stick the flies. Today you can buy rotators that will run from about one to twenty rpm and operate on batteries or AC. The purpose of these devices is to prevent sags and drips of the epoxy and to hold the fly horizontal so that the epoxy will not run and fill the hook eye. Note that you can coat and protect the fly head along with any self-stick or painted eyes that you have placed onto the head.

**Tying down multiple materials.** One way to save time when tying simple flies is to tie down several materials at once. Naturally, this can occur only when two or more materials are going to be placed in the same spot on the hook, such as when tying in a body and rib, body and tail, wings and hackle (dries and wets), wing and topping (streamers), and so on. You have to use common sense with this trick. If you tie in duck-feather wings along with a collar hackle on a wet fly, and the wings end up a little cocked or skewed to one side, then you have accomplished nothing. You have only tied a fly that will have to be retied, or one that may not look or work right in the water. Tying down two materials at once will not work on every fly, but it can save a little time on some patterns.

Tying down the rib and body of a simple wet fly. Tie in the rib at the rear, but attach the body material in the center of the hook shank so that the body can be built up a little more there and tapered at the rear.

One easy way to save time is to hold two materials together—such as this chenille and rib—and tie both in place at once.

**Making neat heads.** Neat heads are desirable on all flies, even simple patterns. Often, the best method is to use the fewest possible wraps when tying down the materials that have to be secured under the head, and then making the thread wraps as neat and small as possible, tapered from front to back. The secret to this is to make nice parallel wraps around the head at right angles to the hook shank, so that each thread wrap lies parallel to the previous one, rather than crisscrossing around the head like a ball of string. The secret also is in making a neat whip finish. For this, I prefer making two whip finishes, each with a few (two to four) wraps around the thread and hook shank, and each pulled up tight and worked tightly into the head. I find this neater than and preferable to tying a single whip finish with eight or ten wraps. Another tip in making a whip finish is to use a bodkin to hold the loop of thread as you pull the working part tight so that the thread will not twist and bunch up, making it difficult or impossible to complete the wrap.

**Tying in weed guards.** I am convinced that the best weed guards on flies that need them are two continuous loops of mono, the two loops bracketing and protecting the hook point regardless of how the fly slides across a snag or weed. Depending on the size of the fly, use 20- or 30-pound-test mono, either the standard type or hard mono such as the Mason brand. The easy way to do this is to cut two strands of mono, each about 3 inches long, and hold them over the hook shank with one strand on each side of the hook. Make sure that the natural curl of the mono (from being stored on a spool) is down so that the pieces will naturally curve around to protect the point. You can hold these in place while also holding the tag end of the working thread, and then begin to wrap the thread around the hook shank and the two strands of mono. This secures the mono weed guards at the rear of the fly at the same time that you are tying the working thread to the hook. Begin at the middle of the hook shank and work the wrap toward the rear, simultaneously binding the thread to the shank and attaching the pieces of monofilament to the hook. Finish the fly, and then pull the ends of the weed guards to the head and tie them down before whip-finishing the thread.

**Thread bodies.** You can avoid adding body material by using the working thread to make a body. To do this on a tailless fly, tie on the thread at the head of the fly (behind the hook eye) and then wrap evenly down the hook shank to the bend. At this point, reverse direction and wrap back up to the head of the fly to tie on wings or other parts. The thread will make the body of the fly. This is a method that is used to tie many tiny flies such as midges and tricos, but you can also use it for larger flies. The thread must be the color you want for the body, unless you use white thread that can be colored with a felt-tip marker.

**Veiled wings on streamers.** One way to make a simple streamer is to forget adding a body, and veil the hook shank with the wing. Instead of mounting the wing material on top of the hook shank, make a wing that encircles the shank to hide it. To do this, tie on the thread in back of the hook eye, then clip the excess thread. Place the wing material on top of the hook shank and make two loose wraps of thread up and over the hook

To make a streamer's wing veil or surround the hook, first tie down the material with soft wraps of thread.

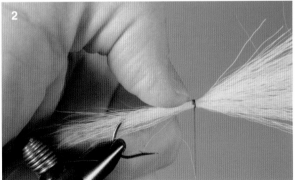

Use your thumbnail to push down on the base of the wing to force the material to encircle the hook shank.

3

Continue by making tight wraps to secure the wing, and then clip the excess material in front of the wrap.

shank and wing material. Then, with the thread snug but not tight on the wing, use your thumbnail to push down on the wing to push the butt ends around the hook shank. The first few times you do this, turn the vise jaws (if you have an adjustable or rotating vise) to check all sides of the fly. Once you are sure that the wing material veils both sides of the the hook, pull the thread tight, make a few more wraps, trim the front end of the wing, and complete the fly. The result is a one-material, super-simple streamer.

**Felt-tip pens to color materials.** Felt-tip pens with permanent ink have long been used to color parts of flies. You can do this on almost any part of a fly.

Markers with fine tips are best for most small flies, while the larger markers are better for big saltwater flies. Permanent markers let you make a fly almost any color. You can use white thread and then color the head black with a black marker. You can make a cream-colored nymph body of floss, dubbing, or yarn, and then color the back with a dark olive, brown, tan, or black felt-tip marker. Always try this on one fly first to see how much the ink bleeds to other parts of the fly. Some markers are advertised as non-bleeding, but check them first.

Use large markers to add color to the wings of large saltwater flies tied with wings that veil the hooks. Materials such as Super Hair, Neer Hair, Aqua Fiber, and similar synthetics produce shiny, bulky flies that simulate a variety of baitfish. A very simple, one-material streamer colored with permanent markers can catch a lot of fish.

Mark the top of the wing with darker colors to simulate the markings and shading of live bait. For instance, the fly might have a white, yellow, cream, shad, or similarly light-colored wing with a back marking of dark blue, black, dark green, or gray. This will result in a pronounced separation of light and dark colors between the belly and the back of the fly.

You can also use markers for more subtle shading, starting at the center of the wing and using successively darker markers as you work toward the top of the wing. You might start with light shades of blue, tan, or green, then progress to medium shades, and finish with darker shades and a black streak along the top.

Markers also let you add spots and stripes to simulate the markings of shad and other fish. You can make light shad-colored or white flies with spots and thin vertical stripes to simulate pinfish, or darker flies with wider stripes to simulate bluegills, or deep yellow flies with brown stripes to simulate yellow perch. Spots and vermiculations along the back

One way to make simple flies is to tie a basic fly or series of flies in a light color and then use permanent felt-tip pens to color the fly. This bucktail has been colored along the back to make the shading often found in baitfish.

You can also use several pens to shade a fly by using dark colors on the back and progressing to lighter shades on the belly.

To add spots such as those on small shad and other fish, use fine-tipped permanent markers.

Stripes like those on yellow perch and other striped batifish are easy to make by dotting the fly.

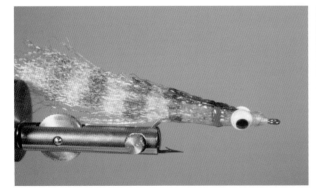

Stripes made with permanent markers can add realism to a simple fly or make the fly easier for fish to see.

Vermiculations and similar markings along the back of a fly are easily added with a felt-tip pen.

To make a "bleeding" fly, use a red felt-tip pen to make blood marks from the gill area and along the belly. This will make the fly seem injured.

can turn a big, simple fly into a good imitation of a small mackerel or bonito. Save the fancy artwork for large flies; on a small streamer, lots of stripes and squiggles often end up looking like a blob of color.

Use a red marker to make a light-colored fly appear to be bleeding and therefore an easy target for any gamefish. The best way to do this is to use a lot of red around the gill area or on the lower belly and tail area of the fly to make it look like an injured fish. Since game-fish are predators and predators are always after the injured, sick, crippled, and slow, red markings can help trigger strikes.

The best way to make these markings on streamer flies for warmwater and saltwater fishing is to lay the fly down on a piece of scrap paper, then mark one side of the fly with the felt-tip marker. Turn the fly over and then mark the other side the same way. Change paper frequently so as to not soil a fly with wet ink that accumulates on the paper.

**Combining tails and wings on dry flies.** One famous fly developed by Harry Darbee (see chapter 3, "Simple Dry Flies") utilizes only two hackles. One hackle becomes the tail, body, and wing, and the second feather becomes the hackle. The technique for making the tail, body, and wings is to clip the tip out of the hackle feather, hold a few end fibers for the tail, and then stroke the rest of the fibers down and tight to the center stem to make the body. Tie the body in place on the hook. Use the tying thread to prop up the forward-pointing fibers to make the wings, and then clip the excess part of the feather. Wind a hackle to complete the fly. The result is an extended-body mayfly imitation. You can do the same thing on a fly to which you also add body material over the forward part of the body to make a "semi-extended body" mayfly, still using the forward part of the feather to make the two wings of the fly. You can use any type of hackle feather or wood duck or similar feathers that make nice tails and attractive mottled wings.

**No-wing wet flies and dry flies.** Tying wet flies and dry flies without wings will not usually adversely affect your fishing success. In fact, it will seldom affect it at all. The reason is that the top part of a dry fly is the first thing that will come into a trout's window of view, which means that the hackle wrapped around the hook shank will often appear to the trout as the wings of a dun or spinner. Among wet-fly anglers, there is increasing interest in the soft-hackle style tied without wings, but with a few long, soft hackle fibers for maximum action in the water. In both cases, the tying is simple.

Tie dry flies by starting at the tail or body, completing the fly up to the hackle, and then wrapping the hackle. You are just avoiding tying the wings first before going on to the next steps. On wet flies, avoid the wings so that all you need to do is to tie in the body and then tie on and wrap the hackle.

**Thread ribs.** The ribs on streamers, wet flies, nymphs, and some dry flies have several purposes: to create flash (tinsel), to add a slight amount of weight (wire), to create an appearance of segmentation in the body, to help protect the body from damage, and to make for a more lifelike appearance. One way to get a ribbed effect (but no weight or flash) is to make a rib with the working thread. It works fine for simple segmentation of the body, and also protects the body materials.

Tie on at the rear of the hook shank. Wrap the thread around the hook shank and the excess tag end until you reach the tail end of the shank. Make sure that you tie on with about 6 to 8 inches of excess thread or tag end. Then, when you reach the end of the hook shank, leave the excess thread while you tie in the tail and body material. Once you have wrapped and secured the body material, follow with the tag end of the thread, using it as a rib around the body. You can wrap the rib in the same direction as the body (up and over the hook shank) or in the opposite direction (up and toward yourself). Reverse-wrapping the rib is better if you want the maximum segmented look or if you are using a soft or full body material in which the rib might disappear if wrapped in the same direction.

To use the working thread to make a rib, leave a long tag end. You can color it with a felt-tip pen to make a dark rib.

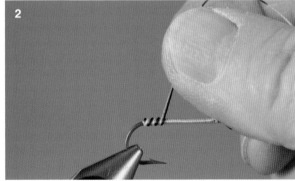

To use the rib and working thread to make a striped body, darken the ribbing thread (the tag end) and then wrap it and the working thread together up the hook shank.

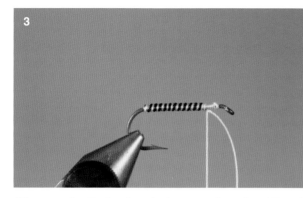

After wrapping the two-tone body, secure the colored thread with the working thread.

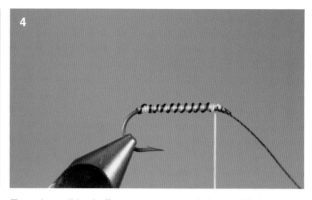

To make a ribbed effect, wrap a smooth base with the working thread and then spiral-wrap the tag end that has been colored with a felt-tip pen.

Coloring the tag end of the thread and wrapping it with the working thread or as a rib lets you make flies that have the same striped effect as quill-body patterns.

**Coloring thread to make heads and ribs.** You can save time by using a light-colored thread and then marking it where and when desired with a permanent felt-tip pen. For example, if you are tying a fly that calls for a white head and a black rib over a light-colored body, you can use white thread for the entire fly. Leave a long tag end when you attach the thread to the hook. Color this tag end with a black marker. Make the fly's body with either the tying thread or another material (floss or yarn, for instance). Then spiral the black-colored tag end around the body to make the contrasting rib before tying it off at the head of the fly.

You can color the head of a fly several different ways. One is to color the thread with a marker before wrapping it to form the fly's head. The second possibility is to complete the head of the fly and then completely color it with a felt-tip marker. A third way is to use the felt-tip marker on only the top of the head to make a head that is dark on top and light on the bottom. This last method is particularly good when tying flies that represent creatures that have white or light bellies and dark backs. If you carry a few permanent markers in your vest, you can even customize flies in the field.

**"See-through" materials.** Use materials that when wet will allow underlying colors of thread to show through. For example, white EZ-Dub becomes translucent when it's wet to allow underlying colors to show through, giving the appearance of the translucent body of a natural insect larva. To take advantage of this, begin with white thread, leaving a long tag end for a rib. Tie in a piece of EZ-Dub and wrap the thread evenly forward to the head of the fly. Color the thread-wrapped hook with a red felt-tip marker, and then wrap the body. The red thread will show through the EZ-Dub when the fly is fished. To finish the fly, color the tag end of the thread dark brown or black and spiral it around the body to make a contrasting rib. As a final touch, mark the head of the fly with a black marker.

**Substitutes for dubbing.** Use yarns and other materials in place of dubbing. I particularly like EZ-Dub from Gudebrod, although there are other, similar products available. The advantage of EZ-Dub is that it comes in both regular and large diameters, and in eleven colors for freshwater flies and an additional five bright saltwater colors in the large diameter. Another good subsitute for dubbing is Angler's Choice Leech Yarn, a long-fibered, shaggy material that makes ideal leeches. When wrapped around a hook shank, these materials resemble dubbing twisted on thread or held in a loop; they produce a very natural, buggy appearance. But you can handle EZ-Dub or Leech Yarn as you would a piece of chenille or knitting yarn, and it will not pull apart or fray out as some other products tend to do.

I also use a lot of yarn, both from fly-tying sources and from craft and sewing shops. Yarn is available in a wide variety of styles, from very bulky to very thin, and from fuzzy styles to the tight, twisted yarn used for macramé work. Thanks to the many colors available and the low cost of craft-store yarns, you can tie a lot of flies for very little money. Often the best way to buy yarn is to split skeins with other tiers. For a few dollars, each of you can have a good supply of body materials in a variety of colors.

Yarn or stranded dubbing materials simplify making two-material wet flies such as this one. To make a tapered body, tie in the body material at mid-shank and wrap it forward, then to the rear, and then forward again. The result is two layers of material at the rear of the fly and three layers in the forward part of the body.

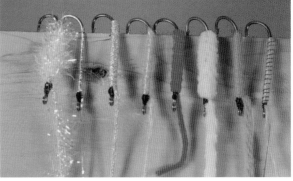

Examples of just a few of the many materials that can be used for fly bodies to create a variety of looks. Left to right: Cactus Chenille, tinsel, braid material, EZ-Dub, Ultra Chenille, chenille, yarn, and EZ-Dub ribbed with the tag end of the thread.

SIMPLE TYING STEPS, TIPS, AND TRICKS

**Making mono eyes in bulk.** Some of the flies in this book require or benefit from eyes made of melted monofilament. Heating the ends of a piece of mono with a flame makes the plastic melt and ball up to form a little dumbbell, which, when tied to a fly, becomes a pair of insect or crustacean eyes. Most of my eyed patterns are saltwater flies, but you can do the same thing on freshwater flies by using very fine mono to make tiny eyes.

If you make your own mono eyes, you have no cost other than the time that it takes. If you make them in bulk, then you can produce enough eyes for dozens or hundreds of flies in a single session, making your fly tying simpler and faster.

Straight melted-mono eyes work on some flies, but others require eyes on horseshoe-shaped stalks. I use such eyes on crab flies tied to swim or crawl sideways (as real crabs do). To make eyes with U-shaped stalks (actually, the stalk is slightly more than a semi-circle), you will need a wood dowel that's about three-fourths the diameter of the horse-shoes that you want to produce. The reason for using a small dowel is that the loops of mono will relax and expand slightly when removed from the stick. I find that dowels from 3/16 to 1/4 inch are about right, but you can use a smaller or larger diameter as required. Cut a slit in each end of a piece of dowel about 12 inches long. Use 50- to 100-pound-test mono, depending on the size of the eyes that you want. Slip one end of the mono into the slit at one end of the dowel and then wrap the mono around the stick in tight coils. Wrap the entire stick this way, and then insert the mono into the slot at the other end. Clip the excess.

Place the entire stick in a pot of boiling water for a few minutes or until the mono has time to absorb some hot water and take on the round shape on the stick. To set the coils of mono, remove the stick from the boiling water and place it in a container of ice water. Remove it after a few minutes and then carefully cut the mono along the length of the stick to to produce a bunch of little circles. To turn the circles into horseshoe eyes, melt the cut ends to form little balls (a candle works fine). If the balls do not darken from the candle flame, you can darken them with a large felt-tip marker. Cut an X into the tip of the marker so you can rotate each little ball inside the X to blacken it.

On shrimp patterns and some other flies, you might want eyes with V-shaped stalks. Follow the same procedure, but wrap the mono around a wide metal ruler instead of a dowel. Heat the mono in boiling water, set it in ice water, and then cut along one edge of the ruler to make a bunch of V-shaped pieces. (If the ruler is very wide, you can cut along both of the flat sides to make two sets of eyes from each wrap of mono.) Melt the ends of the stalks with a candle and darken them with a black marker to make eyes on V-shaped frames.

**Making cloth or vinyl bodies.** Cloth-backed vinyl and clear or translucent vinyl make ideal materials for some flies. You can also use Ultra Suede, Pleather, Bug Skin, or similar materials in the same way. The main purpose of these materials is to make backs, shells, carapaces, and abdomens of flies designed to imitate crabs, shrimp, crayfish, hellgrammites, and similar hard-shelled baits.

For crayfish, hellgrammites, and crabs, the best material is an opaque sheeting, such as cloth-backed vinyl, Pleather, or Bug Skin. For crayfish, do not use a template, but instead cut the material into a slightly tapered rectangle for tying down as a carapace and claws. Cut the material into small pieces appropriate for the size of the fly you are tying, and tie the rectangle down as the last step to make the carapace. You can also cut the rectangle into a tapered coffin shape (tapered at both ends) with cut-outs and such to make for a more natural carapace. This will take more time, which partly negates the idea of simple tying. Fish won't care about exactly how the carapace looks, provided they think that it looks like a meal.

On a shrimp fly, cut the material into the same shape as for a crayfish, but use translucent vinyl. This material is similar to the clear vinyl used for upholstery covers and the windows in folding boat tops. It's available in clear and colors such as rose, yellow, green, and blue. It will create a transparent, life-like look on any fly when tied on top of other body materials. As on a crayfish pattern, the vinyl carapace is tied down last over the other materials to finish the fly. On simple flies, these sheet materials are tied over a palmered hackle or Cactus Chenille that simulates the swimmerets and gills of a crayfish or shrimp. The vinyl carapace makes for a somewhat realistic pattern tied with only a few materials.

An easy way to make crab bodies from cloth-backed vinyl is to use a plastic oval template from an office-supply store. These templates (usually called ellipse templates) include different sizes and shapes of ovals, from almost round to very elliptical. Use a pen to outline the shape on the vinyl material, then cut out the ovals as needed. Use the same template to cut out smaller ovals in a light color (cream or light tan is good) to make the bellies of crabs. To keep from marking the outer surface (although the fish won't care), draw each oval on the underside of the material so that it will be hidden when you tie the fly. To make the crab, glue these parts onto the fly, top and bottom, using Ultra Flex, Pliobond, epoxy, or super glue (CA adhesive). To secure the parts while curing, use tiny spring-loaded clothespins designed for doll clothes.

Note that you do not have to buy an entire yard of material when purchasing this vinyl. While it comes in 36- to 54-inch widths, you can buy as little as 1/8 of a yard. That has been true in all of the craft and fabric shops that I have frequented. An eighth of a yard gives you 4½ inches times the width—still an awful lot of material for very little money.

**Adding flash material the simple way.** Tiers often attach material such as Flashabou or Krystal Flash by first clipping a bundle for one side of the fly and tying it in place on the wing, and then clipping an equal bundle for the other side and tying it in place. A simpler, faster, and better way is to clip a bundle twice the length you need for one side and tie it at the middle along one side of the wing. Then twist and flip the remaining material over the head of the fly, hold it in place on the far side of the wing, and bind the flash in place. Check to see that the flash is in the proper position on each side of the wing before finishing the fly. This simple trick ensures that both bundles will be equal in length and contain the same number of fibers.

To easily tie in flash material, cut a bundle twice the length needed, and then attach the bundle in the middle on one side of the fly.

Pull the rest of the flash material over to the opposite side. Tie it down to cover the far side of the wing.

The completed fly will have exactly even amounts of flash on each side.

**Working with body tubing.** Woven tubing such as Corsair or E-Z Body makes for neat, simple, minnow-like heads and bodies. To use this kind of tubing, cut the material to length to fit onto the hook. If you want to make a flat body, first place the material on a hard surface (such as a kitchen counter) and iron it under medium heat. Then cut it to length. To avoid having to attach the thread to the hook twice, slide the tubing onto a long-shaft bobbin. Then attach the thread to the hook and tie down the wing material. Slide the tubing off the bobbin shaft and onto the hook shank and over the wing material. Tie down the front end of the tubing to make the minnow's head, and then whip-finish the thread.

If you want to use the tubing as body material, begin the same way, with a piece of tubing on the bobbin. Attach the thread at the rear of the shank, and leave a 6- to 8-inch tag end. Slide the tubing off the bobbin and onto the hook. Use the long tag end of the thread to secure the rear of the tubing. Then tie down the front of the tubing and add the wing materials.

**Working with Mylar tubing.** Mylar tubing is a thin, braided material. It is opaque, unlike the woven tubings, and it is often used to make shiny bodies on flies. To use Mylar tubing, first pull out the cord in the center of the braid, and then cut the tubing to length for the hook. Slide the Mylar tubing onto the bobbin shaft. Attach the thread at the rear of the hook, leaving a long tag end. Tie in any tail or underlying body materials. Then slide the tubing off the bobbin and onto the hook shank, and tie it down with the working thread at the front and the tag end of thread at the rear. Complete the rest of the fly with any additional throat or wing materials.

chapter

## BASIC DRY FLIES SIMPLIFIED

A classic dry fly of the Catskill school has a tail, body, wings, hackle, and sometimes a rib around the body. Some are more complicated, with two-color hackles, fancy wings, or complex bodies such as the herl-and-floss construction of a Royal Coachman. Dubbed bodies look nice, but add to the complexity of a fly and the time needed to tie it. Most standard dry flies can be simplified through one of several means.

Let's assume a traditional fly with four parts—tails, body, wings, and hackle—and basic tying steps. The easiest simplification is to tie the same fly without the wings. This preserves the basic style and look of the fly, but spares the tier the trouble of making the wings.

A second possibility is to tie the fly without the usual body, instead using the tying thread as the body material. This approach requires tail material with butts long enough so that the thread can wrap over them not only at the end of the shank, but also over the full length of the hook shank to make an even, smooth body, including the wrap over the butt ends of the wings (if the fly has them).

A third method is to use both the working end of the thread and the tag end to get a striped effect like that of a Quill Gordon's or Red Quill's body. For this simple technique, use white or a light-colored thread such as cream or light yellow. Attach the thread and tie in the tail while leaving a long tag end. Then color the tag end of the thread black or brown with a felt-tip marker. Once the ink dries, hold the tag end and working thread together and wrap both, side by side, up the hook shank and over the butt ends of the tail. At the point where the hackle is tied in, secure the dark tag end and clip the excess thread. Then finish the fly with the hackle. If you want the head to be black, color the thread or the finished head with a black marker before sealing. The result is a striped body very similar to a quill body, but made without the nuisance of stripping the quill to prepare it for tying. An alternative is to wrap the hook shank with the light thread to make the body, then use the tag end, dyed black, to spiral up the body to get a striped effect.

The point is that you do not need a "complete" or standard dry fly to catch fish. In his autobiography, Frederick M. Halford, long regarded at the original missionary of dry flies and dry-fly fishing, noted one trip on which he and a companion (George Selwyn Marryat) found out early one morning that they did not have the dry flies necessary for the day's fishing. They set up an assembly line in which Marryat tied in the wings while Halford completed the flies with tails, bodies, and hackles. It later occurred to them that in his sleepy state, Halford had completed the flies without adding the bodies. The dozen accidents were dubbed "ghost" flies. They later proved to be just as successful as standard dry flies. Both men continued to use "ghost" flies for a time thereafter, though they ultimately abandoned them because it "offended their taste."

"What a strange conclusion for such a wonderful discovery!" noted Vince Marinaro in his brief discussion of this event in his book *A Modern Dry Fly Code*. "It is likely that two more skilled or more observant dry-fly anglers than Halford and Marryat never lived, yet neither of them caught the significance of this important revelation," continued Marinaro. Dry flies, without all the parts, obviously *do* work.

Example of a dry fly without a body. What appears to be the body is really just the butts of the tail material spiral-wrapped with thread. The fish don't seem to care.

Example of a dry fly tied with a thread body and then ribbed with the colored tag end of the working thread.

This simple three-material dry fly is tied with a tail, a body of stranded dubbing material, and a hackle. Many materials and colors can be used for flies such as this.

Example of a dry fly with a coarse thread body, tails, wings, and hackle. The fly has three materials plus the working thread.

Other variations of dry flies can be tied with only a few materials. For example, you can tie a dry fly without hackle if you splay the wings into a spent or almost spent style and use a buoyant material for the body. The spent or nearly spent wings keep the fly upright and let it ride in the surface film Comparadun-style, rather than cocked at an angle like a classic dry fly. Possibilities for the body include some natural furs that are water repellent or resistant. You can also make bodies with closed-cell foam.

Like most other kinds of flies, drys can be simplified in many ways. Simple dry flies might not have all the elegance of fancier patterns, but they catch fish.

## BASIC BODYLESS DRYS

One way to check out how a dry fly looks to a trout is to place a mirror at a 45-degree angle in an aquarium, and then float a dry fly on the surface and study it in the mirror. If you have a bubbler in the aquarium to create some surface ripples, you can even see how the fly would look in fast water. If you do this, you will also see that the main impression of a dry fly, particularly as it comes into view of a trout, is the dimpling of the surface caused by the tails and hackle. Many books on trout fishing have covered this aspect of a trout's vision thoroughly, showing what comes into the fish's view first and how refraction affects what a trout sees. While this does not mean that the size, shape, or color of a fly's body is not important, it does mean that in many cases the body is perhaps less important than we think or suspect. Remember that the flies accidentally tied without bodies by Halford and Marryat resulted in catches just as good as drys with bodies, according to their own accounts.

You can make a simple dry fly by tying on at the head, attaching the wings, spiraling the thread back to tie in the tail, and then working forward to tie in the hackle and finish the fly. Make the butt ends of the wings and tail fibers long enough to fill up the shank length of the hook. This way, when you attach the tails, you can spiral the thread forward so that the tail and wing materials show through the spiral wrapping to create the appearance of a body. The spiral wrap will work as a rib to create segmentation. An alternative is to completely cover the tail and wing butts with thread so that you get a one-color body.

Thread-body drys are not tremendously different from standard patterns, but they do save some time by eliminating the need to make a body with dubbing or a stripped quill.

### Basic Bodyless Dry—Cream

**Hook:** Dry fly, size 8 through 18.
**Thread:** Brown. The thread will make a rib over the long butts of the cream tail fibers, which will serve as the underbody.
**Wings:** Wood-duck or mallard flank.
**Tails:** Cream hackle fibers.
**Body:** The butts of the tail fibers, with a spiral wrap of thread over them.
**Hackle:** Cream or ginger.

First attach the wings, leaving the butts almost as long as the hook shank. Then spiral the thread to the rear and tie down the tail fibers with a few wraps. If necessary, trim any excess length of the tail and wing butts, then spiral the thread forward over the butt ends to the wing area. Tie in the hackle, wrap it, clip the excess, and tie off to finish the fly.

### Basic Bodyless Dry—Grizzly

**Hook:** Dry fly, size 8 through 18.
**Thread:** Black.
**Wings:** Gray hackle fibers.
**Tails:** Grizzly hackle fibers.
**Body:** Black thread, evenly wrapped.
**Hackle:** Grizzly.

Tie this like the cream pattern, but with a solid thread "bodyless body." Attach the wings in standard dry-fly style, and then spiral the thread back to the tail area and tie in the grizzly tail fibers. Trim and taper the butt ends of the wings and of the tails to make a smooth underbody. Tightly wrap the thread forward to make a smooth, solid black body. Then tie in and wrap the grizzly hackle, tie off the feather and clip the excess, and finish the fly with a whip finish.

### Faux Quill-Body Dry

**Hook:** Dry fly, size 12 through 18.
**Thread:** White, cream, tan, or yellow.
**Tails:** Light hackle fibers.
**Body:** The working thread ribbed with the tag end after the tag has been darkened with a marker.
**Wings:** Wood-duck flank.
**Hackle:** Medium blue dun.

This fly is tied as described earlier, using the darkened tag end of the thread to make a contrasting rib on the pale body. The finished fly looks a lot like a Quill Gordon. Attach the thread with a long tag end. Make the wings and wrap over the tapered butt ends to the end of the hook shank. Tie in the tails. Color the tag end of the thread with a black or brown marker. Holding the working thread and the tag end together and parallel, wind them around the hook shank in a tight wrap to make a striped body. (Or wrap the body and then spiral the colored tag end over it.) Tie off the tag end and clip the excess. Finish the fly with the hackle collar. Darken the head with a marker if you wish. You can tie this style with various colors of tails, wings, and hackle.

## BASIC WINGLESS DRYS

Whether dry flies really need wings has always been subject to conjecture. True, a classic dry's wings extend above the hackle, and thus would be visible to a trout as the fly floats into the the fish's window of vision. But the trout also sees the hackle, since it surrounds the entire front of the fly. It's hard to know which element triggers the strike.

My thought is that the overall size, color, and shape of the fly add up to the take-or-don't-take decision in a trout's brain, and that individual parts are less important than the appearance of the whole fly. I like drys that consist of tails, body, and hackle only, since they are simpler to tie. With a few extra turns of hackle around the hook shank, a wing-less dry closely resembles a winged dry anyway, unless we're comparing it to a fly with wings of a markedly different color than the hackle.

Here is a simple generic fly that can be tied in any color or size.

### March Brown Wingless Dry

**Hook:** Dry fly, size 10 through 20.
**Thread:** Any color, or to match the other materials.
**Tails:** Ginger hackle fibers.
**Body:** Fine cream EZ-Dub.
**Hackle:** Grizzly.

To avoid a lump at the tail end of this fly, tie on just forward of the center of the hook. Attach the tail fibers and body material there, and wrap over both of them all the back to the end of the shank. Then wrap the thread forward, making a smooth underbody. Wind the body material and tie off behind the hook eye, leaving enough space to tie in and wrap the hackle. Add the hackle and finish with a neat head. You can use this same simple method to tie many sizes and colors of drys—everything from black or dark (to imitate a dun just emerging from the water) to sulfur, yellow, cream, and such to imitate the spinner stage.

## BASIC FOAM DRYS

You can tie dry flies without hackles and even without tails and still get them to float. This can be done by using foam for the body of the dry, a technique used on some Western dry flies. Many of these Western styles are more complex than the three-material limit of this book, but you can simplify them. For instance, you can substitute a thin wrap of closed-cell foam for the standard body materials on any larger dry fly.

Even on a fly that has a hackle collar, a foam body provides extra buoyancy on rough water or for very long floats. Simple foam flies have a lot of uses.

One way to make dry flies that will always float is to wrap the bodies with very thin strips of closed-cell foam. The foam will ensure that the fly will float, while also creating a segmented appearance.

Foam-Body Dry No. 1

**Hook:** Regular dry-fly hook, size 8 through 12.
**Thread:** Black.
**Tail:** Hackle barbs in any color.
**Body:** Wrap of thin foam material.
**Hackle:** Any color.

Tie this as you would any standard dry fly, but use a thin piece of closed-cell foam as the body material. Wrap the foam around the hook shank and tie it off before attaching the hackle. To keep the fly simple, don't add wings. If you wish to reinforce the foam body, leave a long tag end of thread and reverse spiral-wrap it over the body as a rib. Sources of body material include thin strips of 1- to 2-mm foam available from fly-tying and craft suppliers. This fly can be tied in any colors you want. If you can't find foam in the right shade, remember that you can tint light-colored foam with a permanent marker.

Simple foam-body dry flies work very well in rough water that would drown traditional patterns.

Foam-Body Dry No. 2

**Hook:** Standard dry-fly hook, size 8 through 12.

**Thread:** Black.

**Wings:** Your choice; wood duck and mallard are good.

**Tail:** Thin, tapered piece of foam, part of which will also form the body.

**Body:** The same piece of foam used for the tail, wrapped around the hook shank.

**Hackle:** Any color.

Attach the wings first. Then wrap to the rear of the hook and attach the tapered end of the foam with a few wraps of thread. The same piece of foam becomes both tail and body. After tying down the tail end of the foam, wind the thread forward to the wings. Then wrap the foam body, secure the foam, and cut off the excess. Wrap a conventional hackle collar. If you want to reinforce the body, leave a long tag end of thread when you begin, and use the long tag to counter-rib the foam after making the body.

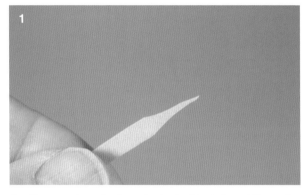

Another way to make foam-body dry flies is to cut the material into thin strips and then taper one end of each strip to make a tail. Tie down the tail and then use the rest of the foam to wrap a body.

A single, tapered strip of foam serves as tail and body on this fly.

This view from above shows the foam tail. It's not elegant, but this style of fly floats very well.

## BASIC BIVISIBLES

In *Flies for Trout,* Dick Stewart describes the Bivisible as a "searching pattern." It is, in that it can be cast almost anywhere to search for trout that might be hiding in places that are not immediately obvious. A Bivisible is also a good pattern for casting to actively rising trout, though its bushy construction often makes this old fly better on fast water or riffles.

The basis of the Bivisible design and indeed the name is that the body is a thick palmer wrap of several brown hackles, with a white hackle in front. Thus, the "bi" or dual visibility—the brown body is visible and attractive to the trout, and the fly's white face is visible to the angler.

Brown Bivisibles are often described in magazine articles and books, but trout like Bivisibles tied in any color. Good colors for the rear of the fly include cream, yellow, tan, ginger, brown, chocolate, gray, black, and both natural and dyed grizzly.

Bivisibles are easy to tie, consisting of only a tail, a body of wrapped hackles (usually brown), and a white front hackle for visibility. They can be tied in any color combination.

Brown Bivisible

**Hook:** Dry fly, size 10 through 18.
**Thread:** Brown.
**Tails:** Brown hackle fibers.
**Body:** Brown hackles.
**Front hackle:** White.

Attach the thread at the rear of the hook shank. Tie in the tail fibers. Attach several brown hackle feathers that are an appropriate size for the hook, and wrap the thread forward. Palmer the brown hackles forward to a spot about one-fourth of the shank length in back of the eye. Tie off the brown hackles and clip the leftover portions. Tie on a white hackle, wrap the thread forward, and finish with several wraps of white hackle.

You can tie Bivisibles in any color combination, including a "reverse" pattern with a white, cream, or tan body and a wrap or two of black or red hackle at the front. Black or any dark color is often more visible than white when the angle of the sun creates a lot of glare on the water. Another variation is to tie a Bivisible with a mix of a grizzly and solid-color hackles. Combining natural grizzly with ginger, tan, cream, black, or gray hackles makes for a subtly mottled or speckled fly. A final variation of this simple fly is to tie it with bright tail and body colors such as red, yellow, light green, chartreuse, orange, or even light blue for panfish and bluegills. Any of these flies will float well, particularly if given a treatment of dry-fly floatant.

## DEER-HAIR DRYS

Deer hair allows for the construction of a lot of simple flies. I'm not talking about stacking or spinning bodies such as that of the original two-color Messinger Irresistible, nor do I mean flies that require a lot of materials or steps. This is a book about simple flies, and within this framework there are flies that do use deer hair. These include flies such as the Comparadun series, Humpies, and Devil Bugs that involve tying down deer hair folded over the hook shank or gathered and bundled to make a different type of floating deer-hair bug.

### Simple Humpy

Simple Humpies can be tied using only three materials. These look a little rough when compared with the original version, but they still float well and take trout.

**Hook:** Dry fly, size 8 through 14.
**Thread:** Black.
**Tails:** Light elk or deer body hair.
**Body:** Floss, covered with an overbody of the remaining elk or deer hair. Floss colors can include tan, red, yellow, green, and lime green.
**Wings:** The butts of the elk or deer hair, tied down after making the overbody, and then raised and divided.
**Hackle:** Dark brown.

Attach the tail first. Pull the butts of the hair out of the way, tie in the floss, and wrap the floss underbody. After tying off the floss and clipping the excess, pull the butts of the elk or deer hair over the body. Tie down the hair butts in front of the floss, and then raise and divide the hair as you would any wing material. Trim the wings to length. Add the hackle collar. You can further simplify the fly by not making the wings. Simply clip the remaining elk or deer hair after tying down the overbody, and then attach and wrap the hackle. Try lots of different underbody colors; they all catch fish.

To make a simplified Humpy, tie in a bundle of deer or elk hair at the rear of the hook, with the tips pointing to the rear. Lift the butts of the hair out of the way, and wrap a body of floss, yarn, or dubbing.

Pull the butts of the hair over the body of the fly and tie them down. Make a few wraps in front of the hair to elevate it.

Trim the hair to length to make wings, and add a hackle collar to complete the simplified Humpy.

Devil Bug

This is a still simpler version of a Humpy. The bundle of hair forms the fly's tails, back, and head.

**Hook:** Dry fly, size 8 through 12.
**Thread:** Black.
**Tails:** Elk or deer hair.
**Body:** Red, yellow, white, black, or green chenille (or any other color you want).
**Back:** The same hair used for the tails.
**Head:** The butt ends of the hair.

The Devil Bug is also known in some areas as a Cooper Bug or Doodle Bug. No matter what people call it, it is nothing more than a simple fly in which the tail is tied on, followed by a body, with the butt ends of the tail hair folded over the body and then tied down and clipped to extend in front of the hook eye. Red is popular, but any color can be tied.

A Devil Bug is a simple deer-hair fly that has been catching fish for decades. Tie down a clump of hair at the rear of the hook. Lift the butts of the hair and wrap a body (red is the traditional color). Pull the hair butts over the body and tie them down behind the hook eye. Tie off the thread and clip the hair so that it extends just beyond the hook eye.

Comparaduns were developed by Al Caucci in the 1960s. The concept was to design a fly that would ride in the surface film, more like a natural mayfly, rather than on the tips of hackle fibers like a Catskill-style dry. The Comparadun also has some of the characteristics of Fran Betters' Haystack, using the buoyancy of deer body hair to float the fly on the surface without the benefit of a hackle. The importance of this is that the fly will imitate more closely the dun stage of a mayfly. You can tie variations of these in many colors. The original had a tail of brown hackle fibers and a body of brown rabbit fur. A simple version with an EZ-Dub body in place of the original rabbit dubbing is shown here.

**Hook:** Dry fly, size 10 through 20.
**Thread:** Dark brown.
**Tail:** Dark dun hackle barbs or brown hackle barbs.
**Body:** Dark brown EZ-Dub or dark brown spun fur.
**Wing:** Dark brown deer body hair, tied in as a wing and spread to a 180-degree arc.

Attach the deer hair, with the tips forward, about one-third of the shank length behind the hook eye. Wrap a bump of thread in front of the deer hair to raise it up, while at the same time spreading the fibers to a 180-degree arc around the hook shank. Then wrap over the trimmed butt ends, wind the thread to the rear, and attach the tails. Tie in the body material, wind the thread forward, and wrap the body material, making one wrap in front of the wing to stabilize it and keep it in an upright position. Tie off the EZ-Dub, clip the excess material, whip-finish the thread, and seal the head. You can tie simplified Comparaduns in many other colors, including black, gray, tan, cream, white, ginger, and furnace.

## SPECIALTY DRY FLIES

Some dry flies don't fit into any category except simple. A couple of them have been around for decades, though many modern anglers don't know about them.

### Neversink Skater

This simple trout fly that consists of nothing but hackle was invented by Edward Ringwood Hewitt in the 1930s. He developed it not to imitate mayflies, caddisflies, or stoneflies, but to imitate butterflies! Although not often remembered today, Hewitt was a well-respected pioneer of American trout and salmon fishing and a serious student of flies, fly tying, colors, the trout's perception of floating and sinking flies, and refraction and reflection of light in the trout's "window." He also made many experiments with rods, reels, and lines. The Neversink Skater is his simple way to imitate the action of a butterfly fluttering on or over the water.

**Hook:** Dry-fly hook of any brand, size 14 or 16. Other sizes will work, but these are the original hooks; Hewitt first tied his Skater on a light, size 16 Model Perfect hook.
**Thread:** Black.
**Hackle:** Two large brown or black dry-fly hackles with very little web.

To tie a Hewitt Neversink Skater, use hackles with very long fibers for the size of the hook. The fly is nothing more than two hackles wrapped face to face in the center of the hook shank. It's designed for skittering and dapping on the water to imitate a butterfly—according to Hewitt.

An example of a finished Neversink Skater, viewed from the front of the fly.

The hackles of a Neversink Skater occupy the center of the hook shank. This simple fly dates from the 1930s.

The hackles are tied face-to-face in the center of a light-wire hook. Secure the thread at the center of the hook shank, and tie in a large hackle with about 1-inch fibers that will make a fly with about a 2-inch diameter. Attach and wrap the feather with the dull or concave side forward. Then attach and wrap a second hackle tied with the dull or concave side facing the rear. The original pattern called for a sparse tie, but you can make Skaters as sparse or as full as you like. After wrapping the hackles, push them together to make one collar, and then tie off the thread. Note that you wrap the feathers in one spot and use your finger- or thumbnail to push the two hackles together to make a tight ruff.

If you go one step further by adding a long tail to the hook before wrapping the two hackles, you can make another fly that is sort of an oversize variant. The addition of this long tail makes a completely different fly, but one that will still alight slowly and gently on the surface to take big trout. Hewitt did note that the addition of a tail does interfere with the movement of the fly on the water.

Hewitt liked brown Neversink Skaters, but you can tie them in any color. Light tan, yellow, light olive, white, and light grizzly are all good choices.

Because of its large surface area and the lightness of the materials and small hook, this fly is difficult to cast with a short leader and line. Hewitt noted that it was best when cast with at least 40 feet of line in the air. This much line also allowed him to drop the fly "like a feather" and then jump and dance it over the water's surface without its getting wet or going under. He found that trout sometimes jumped over or missed the fly when danced this way, and soon discovered that the best technique is to slowly retrieve line to draw the fly slowly over the surface so that the fish can hit it solidly.

### Darbee Extended-Body Mayfly (Two-Hackle Fly)

This fly was the topic of a *Field & Stream* article by Al McClane in 1960. Harry Darbee, the fly's inventor, called it the "two-hackle fly." That's an appropriate name, since it takes only two feathers to make a large but very light dry fly. In his book *Catskill Fly Tier*, Darbee called it "the lightest large fly I had [ever] seen." His extended-body mayfly is a neat pattern and one that can be tied in any color. It is simple to tie and particularly good in small sizes on light-wire hooks. Darbee's Two-Hackle Fly lands gently on the water and takes fish. I've always wondered why it is not more popular and why fly tiers have not come up with more variations of it.

**Hook:** Dry fly, size 8 through 18.
**Thread:** To match the fly.
**Tails and extended body:** Single spade hackle or a hackle with very long fibers at the tip end.
**Hackle:** Regular dry-fly hackle.

The Two-Hackle Fly invented by Harry Darbee consists of one feather that forms the tails, body, and wings, and a second feather that becomes the hackle. Hold the tails/body feather by the tip, with a few fibers pinched between your thumb and forefinger. Fold the rest of the fibers toward the butt to make the body, and bind the folded feather to the hook. To make wings, elevate the excess fibers that are pointing forward.

This top view shows the folded feather that becomes the tails and body. Since it weighs almost nothing, this kind of fly settles to the water very gently. Harry Darbee reinforced the body with rubber cement, but you can omit this step.

Several secrets help to make this fly effective. One is to cut out the tip of the first feather to make divided tails. Hold a few of these fibers with one hand, and pull the rest of the fibers forward along the quill to make the extended body. Tie the tails/body feather to the hook shank a little in back of the hackle/wing position. Darbee applied rubber cement to the body at this point to strengthen and stiffen it, but this can be left out. After securing the body, elevate and divide the fibers pointing out over the hook eye to make the wings. Cut off the rest of the hackle stem. Then tie in a standard dry-fly hackle at this point and wrap it around the hook shank to complete the fly. Clip the excess, tie off the thread, and seal the head with head cement.

You can tie this design with different feathers and on different sizes of hooks to match the hatch. I particularly like it with lemon wood duck for the tails and body, which makes a pretty Light Cahill.

chapter

## BASIC WET FLIES

When I first started trout fishing, my mentor gave me a few wet flies that were the ultimate in simplicity. He called them Gray Nymphs, but they looked like soft-hackle flies. Each one had a spun-fur body and a hackle collar. During the years when I was developing trout-fishing skills, they were my most effective flies.

At one time, wet flies were more complex than they are today. Often a recipe would include a tail, body, rib, throat or hackle, and wings. And that would be a simple one. More complex flies might have a two- or three-part body, or wings of different materials married together (such as the white/red/white of the Parmachene Belle), tags and butts in addition to tails, and hackles of two different feathers.

Today, we have found that simple wet flies work fine. Many consist of nothing more than a body and long, soft hackle, or a body, rib, and soft hackle. The construction is equally simple, and involves just tying on and wrapping the body (and rib, if included), then wrapping a sparse soft hackle and tying off. These flies are typically used for trout and sometimes for Atlantic salmon, though salmon-fishing tradition favors more complex flies.

To make a simple wet fly with only three materials, first tie in the tail. This tail consists of grizzly hackle fibers.

Attach, wrap, and tie off the body material—in this case, chenille. Attach the hackle feather.

Wrap the hackle, tie down the feather, and clip the unused portion. Finish the head and whip-finish the thread.

To make a simple ribbed body, first attach both the body and rib materials to the hook. Wrap the body material and tie it off, and then spiral-wrap the rib.

A rib adds another color or some flash to a simple wet fly.

One simple way to make a sinking fly is to add a bead first, and then tie in and wrap the body material. Finish the body just behind the bead.

Add a throat hackle to make a simple nymph-like fly.

## VARIATIONS

Variations of wet flies are legion. You can do any of the following to a simple wet fly, though eventually you will exceed our definition of a simple fly and begin tying complex patterns.

**Add wings.** Tying a wing or wings to a pattern makes it more like an old-style wet fly. Traditional quill-slip wings can be tied four ways: cocked up and splayed out, cocked down and splayed out, cocked up and curved in, and cocked down and curved in. A simple type of wing is a clump of fibers from a mallard or wood-duck flank feather.

**Add a rib.** Depending on the material, a rib can be simple or complex, and it can add flash, weight, or segmentation to a fly. If you use the tag end of the thread, you are not going to add any weight or flash to the body. If you add Mylar or metallic tinsel, you will get flash, but little weight. You can add wire for weight and also some flash, but both will depend upon the style and diameter of wire that you use. Today, there are a lot of fine, colored wires that will not corrode or dull with use.

**Add a bead head.** A bead, particularly a metal one, will make a wet fly sink faster. You have several types of beads from which to choose. The least heavy are plastic beads. Glass beads are heavier, and metal are the heaviest. You can get beads from all fly-tying shops, and you can find glass and plastic styles in craft and sewing stores. So far, there are no standards as to the size of bead that fits a certain size hook. This is because there are so many different bead manufacturers and also because hooks vary even within a given size. Several nominally size 12 hooks will have different bend styles, barb projections, and wire diameters. Tying with a bead always requires flattening the barb before sliding the bead on the hook. The holes in some beads are larger on one side; usually, the smaller hole goes at the front of the hook shank, behind the hook eye.

## PANFISH FLIES

Panfish wet flies are often simple flies in bright colors, tied with yarn or chenille rather than dubbed bodies. Since panfish such as bluegills, other sunfish, perch, crappies, and other small fish are rarely discriminating about food, you can fish with almost any type of fly. Simple patterns work fine, and they'll let you fill a fly box in relatively little time.

**Hook:** Standard wet-fly hook, size 8 through 12.
**Thread:** Black.
**Tail:** Grizzly hackle fibers.
**Body:** Yellow chenille.
**Hackle:** Grizzly, tied collar style.

This is an example of a basic, simple fly that is ideal for panfish. It can be tied in a number of colors and even with different body materials. When I tie it with floss, I use a throat hackle in place of the collar, since the slimmer body and sparse hackle give the fly a more streamlined, nymph-like look. Panfish like yellow flies, but they'll also eat wet flies tied with white, gray, black, brown, tan, or orange bodies and matching or contrasting hackles and tails.

## WET FLIES WITHOUT TAILS

You can tie any wet fly without a tail. The result is a good fly that looks realistic—wings, body, and hackle—and can be tied in any color and with any materials. You can find more examples of such flies in chapter 7, "Simple Terrestrials." The styles described here often work as wet caddis patterns.

Basic Wet Fly
**Hook:** Standard wet-fly hook, size 6 to 12.
**Thread:** Black or to match the rest of the fly.
**Body:** Yarn, EZ-Dub, chenille, floss, or whatever you like, in any color desired.
**Hackle:** Any webby wet-fly hackle in any color desired.
**Wings:** Matched duck-quill slips. Depending on the pattern, these can be white, smoky gray, slate, red, yellow, black, or brown. The slips can be tied with their points up or down, and splayed in or out.

An easy way to tie in a beard hackle is to turn the hook over. With the hook upside down, you can easily keep the beard centered on the bottom of the shank. A rotating vise helps.

After attaching the beard hackle, return the hook to the normal position to attach the fly's wings.

Tying down wings on a wet fly. Quill-slip wings like these can be angled up or down and tied next to each other or splayed out to give four different looks.

After attaching the wings and trimming the butts, tie in a clump of hackle fibers to make the fly's beard or throat.

A simple, classic wet fly like this is the model for dozens of patterns.

Some anglers contend that splayed wings have more action in the water.

This is a standard wet-fly style that can be varied to create hundreds of patterns. Tails are less important on wet flies than on drys, which typically rely on their tails for some of their flotation.

### Upside-Down Wet Fly

**Hook:** Standard wet-fly hook, size 6 through 12.

**Thread:** Black or to match the pattern.

**Body:** Yarn, chenille, EZ-Dub, or floss in any color.

**Hackle:** Any webby wet-fly feather, tied collar or throat style.

**Wings:** Matched duck-quill slips tied on the same side as the hook point.

The main difference between this fly and the preceding one is that this style is tied upside-down, with the point of the hook between the wings so that the wings protect and hide the point. I have never seen flies tied this way offered for sale, but quill-slip wings are stiff enough to protect the point when you retrieve the fly through snags and weeds, yet they're soft enough to collapse when a fish takes the fly.

The usual way to tie a wet fly is right side up. The body goes on first.

Next, the wings are attached to the top of the hook.

The fly is completed with a throat or beard.

An upside-down wet fly also begins with the body, but the wings go on the same side as the hook point, and the throat goes in the spot usually occupied by wings.

On the finished upside-down wet fly, the wings shield the hook point and make the fly less likely to snag.

Calf tail and other hairs make good wings on simple wet flies. Remove underfur from a hair wing before tying the material to the hook.

If they're tied well, hair-wing wet flies are very durable.

Hair-Wing Wet Fly

**Hook:** Standard wet-fly hook, size 6 through 14.

**Thread:** Black or to match the pattern.

**Body:** Any color or any style of material, including EZ-Dub, floss, yarn, and chenille.

**Wing:** Calf tail, squirrel tail, black bear, or any similarly fine hair that is relatively even in length. Remove any underfur before tying the hair wing to the hook.

**Hackle:** Any webby wet-fly hackle.

Hair wings are perhaps a little easier to attach than wings made of other materials, and they provide a different look. If you go with a very soft fur such as rabbit, the fly will have more undulations and movement in the water, which fish often like. Soft, fluffy furs, however, can be harder than hair to handle and tie down.

### WET FLIES WITHOUT WINGS

The wings of insects that fall into the water are often transparent and virtually invisible. Adding wings to wet flies might not only be unnecessary, but can even make the flies look less like real insects. A simple, two-material fly is often all you need to catch fish.

**Hook:** Standard or 2X-long nymph hook, size 8 through 14.

**Thread:** Black or to match the pattern.

**Body:** Chenille, yarn, floss, EZ-Dub, and so forth, in any color.

**Hackle:** Any wet-fly feather, tied throat or collar style.

This no-wing, no-tail fly serves as a generic style that can be tied in any color with any materials on any size hook. The choice between a throat hackle or a collar hackle is partly subjective, though I generally like throat hackles on sparse, slim flies tied with body materials such as floss or thread. I like the fuller and bulkier collar hackles on fatter flies tied with chenille, yarn, EZ-Dub, and similar materials.

Wet flies made of only two materials—body and hackle— can be tied in any color or color combination. They'be been catching fish for centuries.

Wet flies can be as complex as full-dress salmon patterns or as simple as a shaggy body and a soft hackle. Flies as simple as this one will catch a lot of fish.

# 5

chapter

**BASIC STREAMERS SIMPLIFIED**

Think of a simple, classic streamer and you might envision a Mickey Finn. This fly, popularized by John Alden Knight and named for the drink that supposedly killed the silent-movie star Rudolph Valentino, is a basic streamer. But the original has a tinsel body, a rib, a stacked wing of yellow/red/yellow, and a red throat. It is a six-material fly. We can simplify that by using just a body, a one-layer wing, and a throat; or a body and a double-stacked wing; or a body, a wing, and flash. Any of these is a three-material fly, simple to tie and effective in the field.

Streamer Fly No. 1

**Hook:** Long-shank streamer hook, size 2/0 through 10.

**Thread:** Black or to match the rest of the pattern.

**Body:** Any material that can be tied in at the head and wrapped down, then back up the shank. Possibilities include any color of yarn, chenille, Ultra Chenille, Cactus Chenille, EZ-Dub, tinsel, Mylar, floss, braided or ribbon-style body material, and round braided material.

To make a three-material streamer, start by wrapping the body, and then invert the hook to tie in a red throat.

Return the hook to the normal position. Add the wing (bucktail in this case).

The body, throat, and wing make a simple, effective streamer fly.

**Wing:** Any color of synthetic hair, bucktail, calf tail, black bear, squirrel tail, raccoon, etc.
**Throat:** Red calf tail or red synthetic hair.

This is a basic fly design for everything from trout to tuna. The secret is to use a wing color and shape that will suggest a baitfish, and a body that will reproduce the flash of a baitfish (metal tinsel, Mylar, or a flashy braid) or a lateral line or body color (yarn, chenille, body braid or ribbon, etc.). You can tie this style in sizes, colors, and shapes to represent everything from a black-nosed dace to a pelagic Atlantic mackerel. Remember that you can color the wing with felt-tip markers to simulate bars, bands, vermiculations, or spots.

### Streamer Fly No. 2

**Hook:** Long-shank streamer hook, size 3/0 through 10.
**Thread:** Black or to match the rest of the pattern.
**Body:** Any material that can be tied in at the head and wrapped down, then back up the shank. Possibilities include any color of yarn, chenille, Ultra Chenille, Cactus Chenille, EZ-Dub, tinsel, Mylar, floss, braided or ribbon-style body material, and round braided material.
**Wing:** Two colors of a material such as bucktail, calf tail, or synthetic hair, or a combination of natural and synthetic materials, such as a bucktail underwing and Super Hair overwing.

A two-material or two-color wing obviates adding color with a permanent marker. The simple body can be used for flash or color, as on the first fly. Another difference between this fly and the first is that this one lacks a throat, which some tiers believe simulates red gills.

### Streamer Fly No. 3

**Hook:** Long-shank streamer hook, size 2/0 through 10.
**Thread:** Black or to match the rest of the pattern.
**Body:** Any material that can be tied in at the head and wrapped down, then back up the shank. Possibilities include any color of yarn, chenille, Ultra Chenille, Cactus Chenille, EZ-Dub, tinsel, Mylar, floss, braided or ribbon-style body material, and round braided material.
**Wing:** Any color of synthetic hair or a natural material such as bucktail, calf tail, black bear, squirrel tail, raccoon, etc.
**Flash:** Material such as Flashabou, Krystal Flash, or anything similar tied on each side (see suggestions in chapter 2). Any color or type of flash can be added.

Flash is often a plus when imitating minnows, particularly saltwater species such as silversides and bay anchovies. It also often helps to have the flash extend a little bit (¼ to ½ inch) past the end of the wing, since this flash might suggest scales that an injured fish has lost.

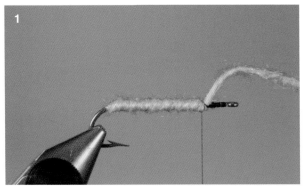

Any body material can be used to make a simple streamer; this is EZ-Dub. Attach the material at the rear of the hook and wrap it up the shank.

Clip the unused body material. Be sure to leave room for the wing.

For the wing, use any natural hair (such as bucktail) or a synthetic material. This wing is Super Hair. Tie the material atop the hook.

Add flash as described in chapter 2. Tie a long bundle on one side of the wing.

Fold half of the material over to the other side and wrap it down so that you have equal amounts of flash on both sides.

Completed three-material streamer with a body, wing, and flash.

**VEILED-HOOK STREAMERS**

Tying a fly so that the wing material veils or surrounds the hook probably originated back in fly-fishing history, but this style has recently become more popular as a simple way to tie simple flies. Forty-odd years ago, I developed a fly that I call the Simple One to take advantage of just this technique. The idea was to create a fly that would consist of just a bucktail wing surrounding the hook shank so that a body was unnecessary. Sometimes I jazz up a Simple One with a contrasting body color, but the original version is a one-material fly.

The lone material—bucktail—is tied on top of the hook with loose wraps and then pushed with the thumbnail so that the hair encircles the hook shank. The finished fly's hook is barely visible. Although I first tied Simple Ones for Chesapeake Bay striper fishing, I've caught freshwater trout, smallmouths, largemouths, pike, bluefish, seatrout, snook, and other species on various sizes and colors of this super-simple fly.

SIMPLE ONE

**Hook:** Regular-length or long-shank hook in sizes 3/0 through 10. For saltwater fishing, use a plated or stainless-steel hook.
**Thread:** Black, white, or to match the color of the hair.
**Wing:** Bucktail or, in small sizes, calf tail. You can also use synthetics such as Sexy Fiber, Super Hair, FisHair, etc. The best colors are the basic shades: white, yellow, chartreuse, tan, black, light green, light blue, and brown.

Attach the thread in back of the hook eye, then prepare and tie down the wing on top of the hook shank, making two loose wraps of thread. Use your left thumbnail to push down on the base of the wing to cause it to encircle the hook shank. Pull the thread tight and add more wraps. Clip the excess wing butts, finish the head, and tie off. Seal the wraps with head cement or epoxy. Variations can include mixing or adding additional colors of wing material, adding a body to the hook shank (chenille, body braid, tinsel, or yarn), adding flash material to the wing, and adding eyes (self-stick, doll, or prismatic). You can use a one-material wing and add bands or bars made with felt-tip markers.

EASY CLOUSER MINNOW

**Hook:** Long-shank streamer hook, size 2 through 12.
**Thread:** Black.
**Underwing:** Squirrel tail or white, yellow, tan, or orange bucktail.
**Overwing:** Squirrel tail.
**Weight:** Lead or lead-free dumbbell eyes.

Begin by tying in the dumbbell on the top of the hook and a little back from the eye. Then add the underwing, tying it down both in front of and behind the dumbbell. Turn the hook over (point up) and tie in the overwing in front of the dumbbell eyes.

This fly obviously runs deep and with its point up. Depending upon the colors used, it can imitate a number of bottom species, including crayfish, sculpins, madtoms, and darters. Variations include coloring the dumbbell eyes and adding a little flash material to the sides of the underwing, as on the original. This is an excellent fly for fresh- and saltwater gamefish.

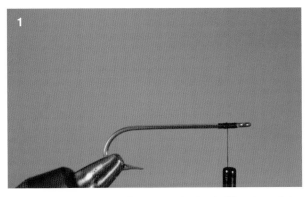

To make a wing that veils the hook shank (like that of the author's Simple One), begin by tying the thread onto the forward part of the shank.

Next, place the wing of the streamer on the top of the hook as you would normally, and make two soft wraps of thread.

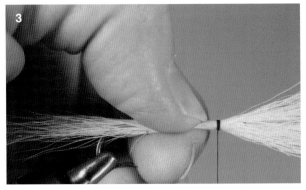

To make the wing veil the hook, push down on the back of the wing with your thumbnail to cause the hair to encircle the shank.

Here, the hair has encircled the hook shank but has not yet been completely secured.

Secure the hair, trim the butts, and finish wrapping the head. One-material flies like this work well in fresh and salt water.

To make a simplified Clouser Minnow, position the hook right side up and attach dumbbell eyes on top of the shank. This will make the fly ride point up.

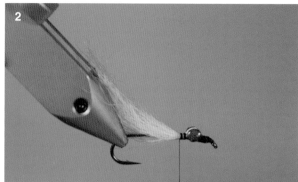

Next, tie on the belly, which will be tied on top of the hook because the fly will ride point up when fished.

Secure the belly hair in front of and behind the dumbbell.

Turn the fly over so that the point is up. Tie on a clump of darker hair to make the back. Clip the excess and finish the head.

Finish securing the hair. Whip-finish the thread and seal the wraps. Experiment with different colors and materials.

## BEND-BACK FLIES

Bend-back flies originated many years ago, when some angler got the idea of bending a hook and tying a bucktail upside down so that the wing hid the hook point. These are simple flies, since most of them are tied without bodies. Bend-backs can be as simple as one material, though they can be made much more complicated. They can also be tied with natural hair or synthetics, and presumably with feathers, though I have never seen them made this way.

### Basic Bend-Back

**Hook:** Bend-back style hook, size 2/0 through 6 (or long-shank hook, bent to shape).
**Thread:** White, black, or any color desired to match or contrast with the fly.
**Wing:** Synthetic or natural hair. Synthetics include everything from FisHair to Super Hair to Sexy Fiber. The wing should be about twice the length of the hook shank. Good natural materials are bucktail, bear, and other long hairs. Comb out the underfur before tying natural hair to the hook.
**Eyes** (optional): Self stick, prism, or doll eyes, glued to the head and then coated with clear epoxy for durability.

Today, bend-back hooks are available from several manufacturers, but you can make your own from any long-shank straight-eye hook. Use needle-nose pliers to grip the hook shank just in back of the eye. Bend the hook slightly. Don't make a severe bend, since this will defeat the purpose and make hooking difficult. You should have about ¼ inch of straight shank behind the hook eye. Since you do not need a body on this fly (it adds nothing), you tie only on this short ¼-inch length of shank.

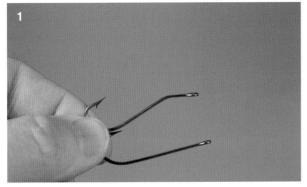

You can buy special hooks for bend-back flies, or you can use pliers to bend a straight-eye hook to this shape. Use long-shank hooks if making your own.

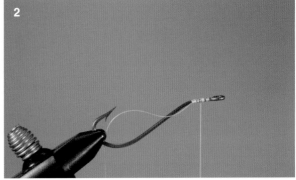

Place the hook in the vise with the point up. Attach the thread on the forward part of the bent hook shank.

Tie down the wing so that the hair extends back over the point of the hook to hide and partly guard it.

Clip the excess hair. You can complete the fly now, or add more materials and flash if desired.

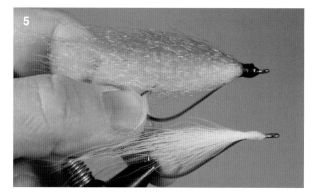

Examples of two bend-back flies, each tied with just one material. The top fly is tied with synthetic Super Hair, and the bottom fly is tied with white bucktail.

Attach the thread and then tie down the natural or synthetic wing material of your choice. You can use any color, though lighter colors simulate natural baitfish better than dark colors. You can also tie in Flashabou, Krystal Flash, or similar materials to add some movement and sparkle. Adding dumbbell eyes is just one variation of this fly. Another is to add prismatic, doll, or 3-D eyes, followed by a coating of epoxy. Place the fly on a rotator until the epoxy cures.

## SHAD FLIES

Most shad flies are simple. They are used to catch both American and hickory shad, which make spawning runs up coastal streams every spring. American and hickory shad are found on the East Coast; only American shad are found on the West Coast. (The American shad were stocked from East Coast fish in the late 1800s.) In the West, American shad are found from Washington down through most of California. In the East, they are caught from New England down to the St. Johns River in Florida. The smaller hickory shad have more scattered populations, occurring principally in New England and the mid-Atlantic regions.

Shad like bright colors, perhaps because bright flies remind them of the krill, copepods, and miscid shrimp that they eat in the open ocean. Most shad flies are tied with only bodies and wings, though some also have throats, and some have tails and ribs. Since these flies are for the most part tied with shorter than normal wings and on shorter than usual streamer hooks (2X long as opposed to 3X to 6X long for most trout streamers), they tend to look shorter and stubbier than most other streamers.

Shad flies can be simple as this two-material pattern with a braided body and calf tail wing. Most shad flies are bright.

### Connecticut River Shad Fly No. 1

**Hook:** Size 2 or 4, 2X to 3X long.
**Body:** Silver tinsel, wrapped to the bend of the hook.
**Wings:** Quill slips from dyed-red duck flight feathers, tied full but short, about half the length of the hook shank.

### Connecticut River Shad Fly No. 2

**Hook:** Size 2 or 4, 2X to 3X long.
**Body:** Gold tinsel, extended around the hook bend.
**Wing:** Orange or yellow, tied short.
This fly is sometimes fished with an orange or yellow bead on the leader in front of the hook.

### Neon Shad Fly

**Hook:** Mustad 7287 double point, size 4 through 8.

**Body:** Colored or tinsel underwrap with overwrap of colored mono such as golden fluorescent, red Sunset Amnesia, or green Trilene XT Solar.

**Wing:** A very few strands of flash material such as Flashabou, Krystal Flash, or a similar product.

The translucent monofilament over the colored underbody makes for a translucent body. The side-by-side shanks of the double-point hook make it easy to tie down the mono; start the forward wrap of the mono by running the mono between the hook bends and wrapping it around the shanks. Sometimes these flies tied on very small hooks (size 10 or 12) will work well for shad and panfish.

### Thom Rivell Shad Fly No. 1

**Hook:** Mustad 34007 stainless steel, size 4 or 6.

**Body:** Silver metallic chenille wrapped on rear two-thirds of the hook shank.

**Head:** Fluorescent orange chenille wrapped on the front third of the hook shank.

This fly resembles the lead-head shad darts used by spin fishermen. Fly tiers make many versions of this basic shad fly by changing colors and materials.

### Zimmer/Swope Shad Fly

**Hook:** Size 6 or 8, 3X long.

**Body:** Standard or fluorescent chenille in white, red, orange, green, or yellow.

**Wing:** White, red, orange, yellow, or green calf tail, tied short (the length of the hook shank). Many tiers use fluorescent hair on these flies. The wing color should contrast with the body.

This fly was developed for mid-Atlantic hickory shad.

### Pfeiffer's Braid Body

**Hook:** Size 6 through 10, 2X long.

**Body:** Any bright braid such as those from Gudebrod or Kreinik. Either round or flat braid will work.

**Wing:** Calf tail or brightly dyed hackle, contrasting with the body color.

The plastic braid gives some color to the body along with a little—but not too much—flash. One material provides the same effect as the tinsel-ribbed chenille bodies of other flies.

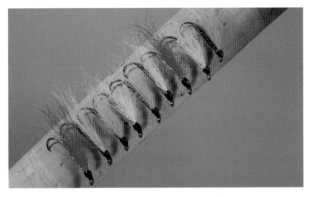

These examples of Pfeiffer's Shad Fly are all tied with a braid material (Gudebrod HT Braid or Metallic Hologram Braid) and calf tail. A shad fly's body and wing should be different colors.

## Shad Shrimp Fly

Some West Coast shad flies are more complicated than necessary, sporting bodies and wings made of several materials. This simple pattern can be tied with any bright material for effective West Coast fishing.

**Hook:** Regular or 2X long, size 4 through 8.
**Thread:** Fluorescent lime green.
**Body:** Lime green chenille or Ultra Chenille.
**Wing:** Lime or insect-green hackle, collar style, with an overwing of a little green flash material.

This three-material fly can be weighted with a cone head, bead head, or dumbbell eyes, and can also be tied without the flash material. Making the standard version involves tying on at the rear, attaching and wrapping the chenille, attaching and wrapping the hackle, and tying on a few pieces of flash material. You can tie this in any color; good shades include fluorescent red, orange, pink, yellow, chartreuse, orange, light blue, and white.

Another simple type of shad fly has a chenille body, flash for a wing, and a wet-fly hackle. Flies can be tied this way in a variety colors and with many materials.

Paradise Beach

This simple, effective fly was designed for shad fishing the Paradise Beach area of the American River on the West Coast.

**Hook:** Regular or 2X long, size 4 through 8.
**Thread:** Red.
**Tail:** Red marabou or red grizzly marabou.
**Body:** Black Diamond Braid or a similar braid material.
**Eyes:** Silver bead chain.

Many West Coast shad flies are tied weighted to get deep in big rivers. Attach the eyes to the hook first. Then wind the thread to the rear of the hook, attach the braid material, wrap the body, and finish the fly by wrapping the braid around the bead-chain eyes. Instead of bead chain, some tiers use a metal bead, a cone head, or dumbbell eyes. You can tie this fly in any color.

## STEELHEAD AND PACIFIC SALMON FLIES

Most flies for steelhead (sea-run rainbow trout) and Pacific salmon are bright, but they don't have a lot of flash that might spook fish. In this respect, they are like shad flies (or vice versa). Fluorescent colors are best, since they are brightest and most easily seen in the stained water that is common early in the season. Traditional materials for the simpler versions of these flies include floss, Cactus Chenille, Estaz, EZ-Dub, chenille, Ultra Chenille, Vernille, yarn, tinsel, and flat and round braided materials. Some steelhead and Pacific salmon flies have a lot of materials and tying steps, but many good patterns for these species fit our definition of simple flies.

Glo Bug, Traditional

**Hook:** Standard length, size 1 through 8.
**Thread:** To match the color of the yarn.
**Body:** Glo Bug yarn tied in place and trimmed. Good colors include white, peach, yellow, orange, red, pink, and similar shades that resemble fish eggs.

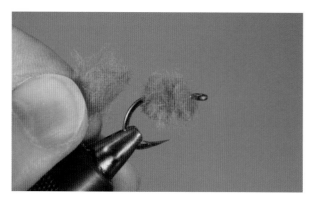

A traditional egg fly consists of Glo Bug yarn tied to the hook and then clipped to resemble an egg or egg cluster.

Attach the thread in the middle of the hook shank, and then add one, two, or three short pieces of Glo Bug yarn. Tie off the thread. Trim the yarn to a round shape to resemble a fish egg. One variation is to tie with a light color, then mark a spot on the egg with a bright felt-tip marker. Other variations are to add a tail or wing of white marabou to resemble milt.

### Glo Bug, Cheater
**Hook:** Standard length, size 1 through 8.
**Thread:** Color to match egg.
**Body:** A ¼- to ½-inch diameter pom-pom (plain or sparkle style) available from craft shops. White, orange, yellow, pink, and red are good colors.

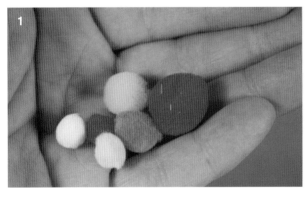

Pom-poms available from craft stores can be used to make egg flies. Many colors and sizes are available.

To make a "cheater" Glo Bug, first wrap some thread onto the center of the hook shank as a base for the glue.

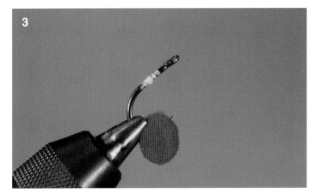

Then position the hook in the vise with the point showing, and carefully impale the pom-pom on the hook point.

Use a fingernail to push the pom-pom into place on the hook, taking care to keep your finger away from the hook point.

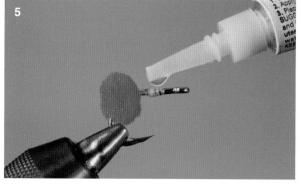

Slide the pom-pom around on the hook shank, and then add cyanoacrylate glue (super glue) to the thread wraps.

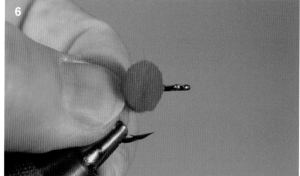

Slide the pom-pom into place on the wet glue. Give the glue a moment to cure.

Cheater Glo Bugs are easy to make in large quantities.

Wrap a base of thread at the center of the hook shank to serve as a gluing base. Hold the hook in pliers or a vise, and *carefully* force the pom-pom onto the hook point and around the bend. Finish by adding some CA glue to the thread base and sliding the pom-pom into place. Variations include using a bright felt-tip pen to add a color spot to the egg. After gluing the egg in place, you can also add a tail of white marabou to simulate milt.

**Hook:** Regular length, size 2 through 8.
**Thread:** Fluorescent orange.
**Body:** Chartreuse or fluorescent green chenille.
**Hackle:** Yellow, palmered over the body.
**Back/shell:** Orange or flame Glo Bug yarn.

This buggy-looking fly works well not only for steelhead, but also for shad, and it can imitate a shrimp for much saltwater fishing. It also works well in small sizes and dark colors for panfish and trout. To tie it, attach the thread, tie down the flame Glo Bug yarn for the back, tie in the hackle, and then attach the chenille body material. Wind the thread forward. Wrap the body forward, followed by the hackle, and tie each off in turn. Finish the fly by pulling the back/shell forward over the body, tying it down, and clipping the yarn to leave a short "head" over the hook eye. A variation is to fold the yarn over the back, tie it down, and then fold it back and tie it down again to make a short wing.

To tie a Fluorescent Wiggler, first attach the back or case of fluorescent Glo Bug yarn or another thick yarn.

Tie in the hackle and the body of chartreuse or yellow chenille.

Continue by wrapping the thread to the front of the fly.

Wrap the chenille up the hook shank to make the body of the fly.

Spiral the feather forward to make a palmer hackle and tie off the feather.

Pull the yarn over the top of the fly to make the back or shell.

Clip the excess yarn and finish the fly's head.

**Simple Rusty Caddis Pupa**

**Hook:** 2X long, size 4 through 8.

**Thread:** Black.

**Body:** Orange-brown or rusty mohair, EZ-Dub, or a similar material.

**Collar:** Brown partridge hackle.

**Head:** Peacock herl, wrapped in front of the hackle.

Attach and wrap the body material, the partridge hackle, and, in front of the hackle, the peacock herl. You can use different colors for the body and even replace the brown partridge with mallard, guinea fowl, grizzly, or a solid-color hackle.

To tie a Simple Rusty Caddis Pupa, begin by tying down a length of brownish yarn, EZ Dub, or mohair.

Wrap the thread and then the body material forward. Tie off the body material. Attach the hackle, leaving a little space so that you have room to add the peacock-herl head.

Wind the hackle around the hook shank and fold it back to make the collar.

Attach a few strands of peacock herl.

Wrap the herl to make the fly's head. Tie off the herl and whip-finish the thread.

### Frammus

**Hook:** 2X to 3X long, size 2 through 8.
**Thread:** Black.
**Body:** Fluorescent chartreuse chenille or Ultra Chenille.
**Wing:** Fluorescent cerise poly yarn, clipped no longer than the shank.

Tie in the body material, wrap it forward after the thread, then tie in a short wing of poly yarn and you have a good fly for steelhead and salmon. It will also work for shad, panfish, and trout. You can use any color, though the original had a fluorescent chartreuse body and a cerise yarn wing. Mix and match other colors, including pink, red, white, orange, light green, yellow, and purple. Variations include making the wing with a short clump of bright calf tail.

### Two-Material Steelhead/Salmon Fly

**Hook:** 2X long, size 2 through 8.
**Thread:** Black.
**Body:** Any bright material; chenille is the standard material.
**Hackle:** Any bright hackle, tied collar style.

This can be tied in mix-and-match colors of white, yellow, pink, orange, purple, red, cerise, light green, blue, and even black. A variation for West Coast rivers and big water is to add a bead, cone head, or dumbbell to the hook before tying. Other variations are to add a palmered hackle, tail, wing, or rib to dress up the fly even more.

chapter

## SIMPLIFIED NYMPHS

The flies in this chapter are not so much copies of a specific family, genus, or even style of nymph as examples of simple, suggestive imitations of the nymphal forms of mayflies, caddisflies, and stoneflies. The aquatic insects that these flies represent are staple foods of trout and staple lures among fly fishermen. You can tie most of these flies in various sizes and colors, and you can modify them by adding weighting wire or bead heads.

### Peacock-Herl Nymph

Peacock herl has colors and iridescence that are particularly attractive to trout. Whether it resembles the natural colors of a live nymph, just looks buggy, or has some other quality is not known, but peacock works. Peacock herl comes in bronze and dark green shades. You can use it one piece at a time or wrap or several strands together if you wish to make a larger or more bulky nymph.

To make a simple peacock-herl nymph, tie on at the rear of the hook shank and add a few strands of peacock herl.

To complete the fly, wrap the thread forward and then wrap the peacock.

Variations of simple peacock nymphs. Left to right: nymph with tails and antennae of peacock; nymph with cone head (beads can also be used); fat nymph (multiple wraps of peacock); and slim peacock-herl body.

**Hook:** Any hook from about size 4 through size 16, from standard length up to 4X long.
**Thread:** Black.
**Body:** Bronze or green peacock herl.
**Head:** Black thread.

You can fill the entire hook shank with herl or tie the fly with a bead head. If you use a bead head, bend down the barb and slide the bead on first and then tie the fly, finishing in back of the bead. You can also tie the fly with a wrap of lead or lead-free wire on the hook shank, or with a tail of peacock. To add a tail, tie in two or three strands of peacock herl at the hook bend so that the tips point to the rear. Advance the thread and then wind the rest of the herl up the hook shank. Tie off the strands of herl at the head of the fly.

Another variation is to tie off the peacock herl at the head with the strands under the fly, angled toward the hook point. Clip the peacock herl to make a short throat that can simulate legs or gills. Even if you add tails or legs, this is still a simple fly to tie.

### EZ-Dub Nymph

EZ-Dub is a Gudebrod product that comes in two sizes and many colors. (There are other brands of similar products, such as Glisson Gloss E-Zee Bug.) As the name indicates, EZ-Dub is a replacement for conventional dubbing materials and traditional techniques. In effect, it is pretwisted, ready-to-wrap dubbing. It does not come apart or separate (as do some products), and it's easy to tie onto a hook. EZ-Dub is no more difficult than yarn to use, yet it has a fuzzy, natural texture that makes for good-looking bodies. The small size can be used to tie flies as small as size 20; the large size makes good bodies on hooks as big as size 2. This material can be used in a number of different ways and combined with a head of peacock herl or a darker color of EZ-Dub. Other products that work the same way are E-Zee Bug and, for an even shaggier appearance, Leech Yarn.

**Hook:** Any nymph hook from size 10 to 20.
**Thread:** Black or to match the rest of the fly.
**Body:** Brown, tan, cream, white, or olive EZ-Dub (small size).
**Head:** Darker EZ-Dub, built up to make for a slightly larger head. An alternative is to tie the body with fine EZ-Dub and the head with large EZ-Dub.

You can tie this fly with a metal bead to add flash and weight. Put the bead on the hook first, and then tie the fly, finishing behind the bead. Gold, copper, and nickel are good colors for beads on these flies.

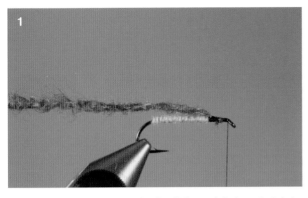

An easy nymph can be tied using light and dark materials to make the head and body. Here, light-colored EZ-Dub has been wrapped on the hook shank and the darker, larger material has been attached to make the head.

A few wraps of the dark material form the fly's head.

Cactus Chenille also works well to make heads on simple, two-material nymphs.

**Basic Nymph**

**Hook:** 2X or 3X long, regular or stout wire, size 6 through 14.

**Thread:** Dark brown or to match the fly.

**Tail:** A short piece of dark brown emu or ostrich herl.

**Abdomen:** Dark brown EZ-Dub.

**Wing case:** A section of black or dark brown duck or turkey quill.

**Thorax:** Dark brown ostrich herl or emu. Emu fibers are longer and coarser than those of ostrich.

This simple nymph can imitate everything from large stonefly nymphs to tiny mayflies. After attaching the thread, tie in the ostrich herl or emu so that it will extend just beyond the hook bend as a tail. Do not clip the excess herl. Then tie in the EZ-Dub and advance the thread two-thirds of the shank length up the hook, wrapping over the herl. Wind the EZ-Dub forward, tie it off, and clip the excess. Attach a section of wing quill so that it points backwards; this will become the nymph's wing case. Hold the emu or ostrich out of the way and wind the thread forward. Wrap the thorax with the emu or ostrich. Fold over the wing case, tie it down, and clip the excess. Finish the nymph's head.

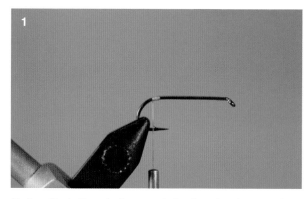

To tie a Basic Nymph, first attach the thread at the rear of the hook shank.

Tie in some emu or ostrich to make the tail. Don't clip the butt ends of the herl; they will become the thorax.

Tie in the abdomen material and wrap the thread forward.

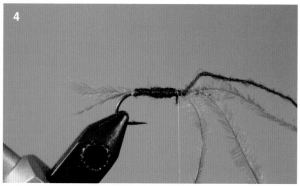

Wrap the abdomen material forward and tie it off. Note that the herl is still attached to the hook.

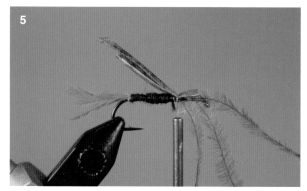

Tie down a section of turkey quill to be folded over and used as the wing case.

Wrap the thread forward and then follow it with the emu or ostrich to make the thorax.

Fold the turkey slip over the thorax area and tie it down.

Finish the fly by clipping the forward part of the turkey and then completing the head. These basic steps, though appearing to make a slightly complex nymph, still use only three materials.

Although it's simple, the finished fly has a distinct abdomen and thorax. The emu or ostrich herl makes a plump, fuzzy thorax, and the individual fibers can suggest the legs or gills of a nymph. Besides dark brown, this fly is also good in black, gray, light brown, and occasionally in cream or tan.

## CRANE FLY NYMPHS

The larvae of crane flies can measure from 1 to 3 inches long. Their colors vary by species from cream to olive. They have been described as looking like sausage links. Crane flies range from streams and rivers to the quiet waters of still ponds. Imitations are easy to tie, and they can be fished anywhere for trout or panfish.

### Teflon-Tape Crane Fly

This simple tie consists of only a wrap of tape and a thread rib.

**Hook:** Any long-shank or curved-shank hook (like that for a swimming nymph or a model such as a Mustad 37160), size 1 through 10.

**Thread:** Black.

**Body:** Teflon plumber's tape wrapped around the hook.

**Rib:** Black tying thread.

An article in *Pennsylvania Angler* shows how imaginative tiers can be with this simple design. Since crane fly larvae are nothing more than long, grub-like or worm-like creatures, you can tie imitations with anything—including the Teflon tape used by plumbers on threaded connections. The rib is the tag end of the tying thread. Nothing could be simpler.

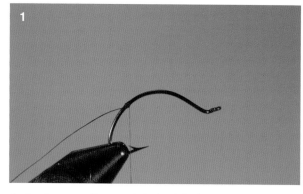

A simple crane fly nymph is best tied on a curved shank hook, such as this Mustad 37160. Leave a long tag end when you attach the thread to the hook.

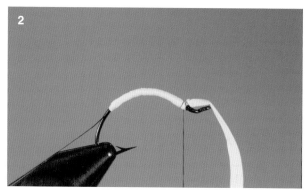

Tie in a piece of Teflon plumber's tape. Wrap the tape forward after winding the thread forward. Note that a long tag end has been left to rib the fly.

Make the rib with the tag end of the thread. Tie off the rib at the fly's head.

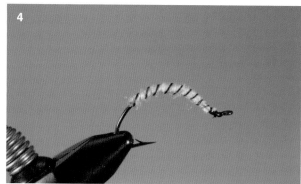

The same type of fly can be tied with EZ-Dub, mohair, dubbing, or yarn.

EZ-Dub Crane Fly Nymph

This looks more like a "real" fly pattern, but it still has only one material.

**Hook:** Any long-shank or curved-shank hook such as a Mustad 37160, size 1 through 8.

**Thread:** Black.

**Body:** White, cream, tan, or another light shade of EZ-Dub or a similar material.

You can also use yarn, fine chenille, Ultra Chenille or Vernille, and even floss for this fly, though you will have to wrap several layers of floss to make a sufficiently thick body. If you use yarn, twist it to make a tight, smooth body rather than a fuzzy one. With any material, the tying procedure remains simple. Leave a long tag end when you attach the thread to the hook. Attach, wrap, and tie off the body material, and then rib the body with the long tag end of the thread.

## CADDIS LARVAE

Caddis, as any entomology or fly-tying book will relate, are aquatic insects that build sand or stick cases during their life underwater. They use detritus from the stream bottom to construct form-fitting "cocoons," in which they live before they rise to the surface to become winged, adult insects.

### Sand-Case Caddis

The fact that caddis make their larval cases from sand and sticks allows you to make very realistic flies. The sand or stick part resembles the case, while the peacock or EZ-Dub head simulates the head of the caddis larva peeking out of the case. Since the sand or stick case is glued onto the hook, this is as much fly gluing as tying. By gluing a bunch of bodies, letting the glue cure, and then wrapping all the heads, you can make a lot of flies in very little time.

**Hook:** 2X long, size 6 through 12.
**Thread:** Black or olive.
**Body:** Sand or very fine gravel.
**Head:** Peacock herl, or black or olive EZ-Dub.

The best way to make these flies is to use an assembly-line process. The best sand comes from the stream where you fish, provided that removing sand from the stream bottom is not illegal. It also helps to roll over some rocks (be sure to roll them back again when finished) and pick up a few sandy caddis cases and drop them into a bottle of alcohol to use as samples for size and style when you are tying. Make sure that the sand is completely dry before using it—you can't glue wet sand.

Mix five-minute epoxy or Ultra Flex, coat the rear two-thirds of the hook, and then roll the hook gently in the sand. If you have a few very small sticks or some leaf mold in the sand, so much the better. I like Ultra Flex (a Scientific Anglers/3M product) because it is tough, flexible, and a tan color that will not look strange should a particle or two of sand fall off, or if the glue shows between the grains. It helps to smooth out the sand on the hook shank, either using your fingers or a popsicle stick. Make sure that the sand build-up does not affect the hook gap.

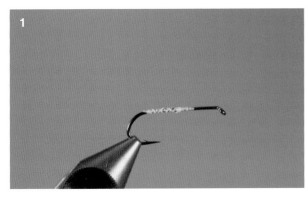

To make a Sand-Case Caddis, first spiral wrap some thread around the rear two-thirds of the hook shank.

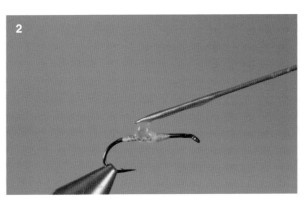

Next, coat the wrapped shank with epoxy glue or Ultra Flex.

While the glue is still sticky, dip the hook into sand.

After the glue has cured, attach the thread in front of the sand.

Tie in one or more strands of peacock herl.

Wrap the peacock to make the head, and then tie off behind the hook eye or between the head and body.

Left to right: Sand Case Caddis with heads of Cactus Chenille, EZ-Dub, emu, and peacock herl.

Set the sand-coated hooks aside. When the glue is cured, clamp a hook in your vise and tie on the thread just in front of the sandy case. Clip the excess thread, tie in a strand of peacock herl, and wrap it around the hook shank in front of the sand to make the larva's head. Tie off the peacock herl and whip-finish the thread. To protect the sand case, coat it with head cement.

### Basic Caddis

This is a traditional style of larva. You can use yarn, EZ-Dub, fine chenille or Vernille, or floss for this easy two-material fly. The head can be tied of peacock, yarn, EZ-Dub, or similar materials.

**Hook:** 2X-long nymph hook or long-shank streamer hook, size 6 through 10.
**Thread:** Black.
**Body:** White, cream, yellow, or tan yarn, chenille, EZ-Dub, or floss. Each body material will create a slightly different look.
**Head:** Peacock herl, yarn, EZ-Dub, mohair, or similar dark materials. The best colors are black or dark olive.

Attach the thread at the rear of the hook, tie in the body material, advance the thread, and wrap the body. After securing the body material, add a short head made of a dark material.

A variation of a caddis nymph can be easily tied using a body of yarn, EZ-Dub, mohair, or similar materials and a head of dark EZ-Dub.

# SIMPLE NYMPHS AND MISCELLANEOUS FLIES

### Bead-Head Caddis

By adding a dark bead to the hook before tying, you eliminate having to wrap the head. This is still a two-material fly, but one with a little weight to get it down where trout will be searching for and feeding on the real larvae.

**Hook:** 2X- or 3X-long nymph model or a long-shank hook, size 6 through 12. The bead is easiest to slide onto a Model Perfect hook with the barb bent down.
**Thread:** Black.
**Body:** Floss, EZ-Dub, chenille, Vernille or Ultra Chenille, yarn, and so forth in white, yellow, tan, cream, and other light colors.
**Head:** Black or dark metal bead.

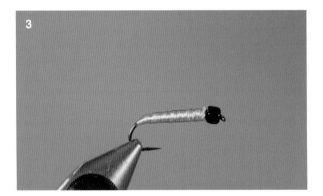

To add weight or a different look to a caddis imitation, use a bead for the head.

Wrap the hook shank with thread and attach the body material at the rear.

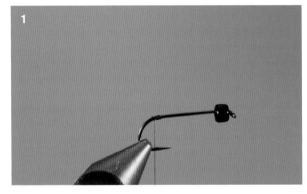

Advance the thread, wrap the body material, and tie off behind the bead head to complete the fly.

First bend down the hook barb and then slide the dark bead in place. You can let the bead slide on the hook as you tie on at the rear, or attach the thread in back of the bead and build up a bump to keep the bead in place. Move to the rear of the hook shank, tie in the body material, and return to the head. Wrap the body material and tie it off with tight wraps of thread immediately in back of the bead. The dark bead will simulate the head of the larva. You can tie dark-colored nymphs the same way, using bright beads for flash as well as weight and making the bodies with olive, brown, gray, and black materials.

## WIRE-BODY NYMPHS

You can tie flies with bodies of wire for color, flash, and weight. Wires in many sizes and colors have become readily available to fly tiers. The advantage is that you get the weight that sinks the fly down to where the trout live, and the colored wire can resemble a number of shiny or iridescent nymph bodies.

### Brassie

**Hook:** Standard length to 2X long, size 12 through 20.
**Thread:** Black.
**Body:** Brass or copper wire the same diameter as or slightly smaller than the hook wire.
**Head:** Peacock or ostrich herl (depending upon size of the fly); on larger Brassies, you can also use mohair, EZ-Dub, or yarn.

To make a smooth body, bind the end of the wire along the length of the hook shank. Attach the wire near the front of the hook, and keep wrapping the thread all the way back to the bend. Then wind the thread forward all the way to the head area. Keep the wire tight as you wind it around the hook to make the body. Tie in the head material and wrap it, finishing with a small head of black thread. If you make the head with yarn or a similar material, pick it out with a dubbing teaser to make it fuzzy. Variations include tying with almost any color and size of wire.

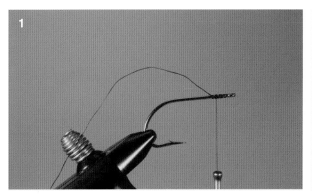

Begin tying a wire-body fly by tying on at the front of the hook. Attach a length of wire (usually brass, but other colors are available) and then wrap over the wire to the rear of the hook.

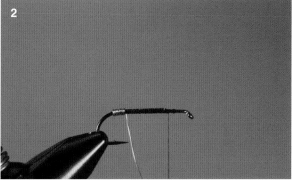

Wind the thread forward and then wrap the wire around the hook shank to make a bright, metallic body.

At the head of the fly, tie off the wire and use wire cutters or coarse scissors to clip the excess wire. Tie in some head material such as ostrich herl.

An example of a typical Brassie with a wire body and a peacock-herl head.

A variety of hooks and head materials can be used to make different wire-body flies.

### WOOLLY WORMS AND WOOLLY BUGGERS

Woolly Worms and Woolly Buggers are simple, three-material flies that are staples for any fly fishing today. The Woolly Bugger evolved from the older Woolly Worm, and differs only in the tail.

Woolly Worm

**Hook:** Long-shank hook, size 1/0 through 10.
**Thread:** Black or to match the fly's color.
**Tail:** A short piece of red yarn.
**Body:** Chenille, with a palmered hackle over the body. Popular colors for both the body and hackle are black, white, olive, dark brown, chartreuse, tan, and gray.

Tie in a short length of red yarn for the tail, and then attach the hackle and the chenille body material. Wrap the thread forward, wrap and tie off the chenille, and palmer the hackle over the body. Variations include using chenille and hackle that differ in color and adding a cone head, bead, or dumbbell eyes to the head of the fly for weight. You can also give the fly a red throat.

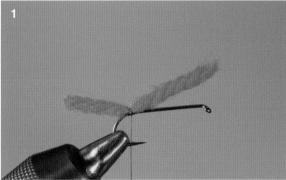

1

To tie a Woolly Worm, first attach the thread and then tie in a length of red yarn.

2

Next, tie in the hackle and the chenille.

3

Wrap the thread forward, followed by the body material.

4

Palmer the body with the hackle and tie off the feather.

5

The completed Woolly Worm is a good, simple fly for trout, bass, and panfish.

6

Follow the same steps to tie a Woolly Bugger, but use marabou for the tail in place of a tag of red yarn.

### Woolly Bugger

**Hook:** Long-shank hook, size 1/0 through 10.

**Thread:** Black or to match the fly's color.

**Tail:** Marabou the same color as the fly's body.

**Body:** Dark chenille with a palmered hackle. Popular colors include dark olive, light olive, brown, gray, black, white, yellow, and chartreuse.

This fly has eclipsed the Woolly Worm in popularity, with the action of the marabou tail making the difference. The tying technique is the same as that for the Woolly Worm; simply replace the red wool tail with a tuft of marabou. The same variations also apply. Most anglers prefer weighted Woolly Buggers; some tiers use weighting wire under the body, while others prefer beads, cone heads, or dumbbells.

## SIMPLE CRAYFISH

Of the 600-plus species of crayfish found in the country, many become fish food. Most crayfish live in the water, where they scurry around on the bottom and can become meals for trout, smallmouth bass, and largemouths. Crayfish range in color from brown to almost black; many species turn reddish orange or brown during the mating season. There are many flies that represent crayfish, but few as simple as this one.

### Pfeiffer's Simple Crayfish

This and the shrimp in chapter 10 are tied similarly, with only the materials and colors slightly different. The dumbbell on this fly makes it a three-material pattern that is particularly effective when tied on a jig hook to remain snagless.

**Hook:** Jig hook, size 2/0 through 6.

**Thread:** Brown.

**Weight:** Dumbbell. The size varies according to the size of the hook and the amount of weight desired.

**Body:** Brownish Cactus Chenille or Estaz.

**Claws and carapace:** Cloth-backed vinyl, Bug Skin, Pleather, or a similar material in brown, reddish brown, orange, dark brown, or black, cut to a Y shape that combines claws and carapace.

First tie the thread to the shank just in back of the sharp bend in the jig hook. Then tie in a lead or lead-free dumbbell so that it will be on the underside when the fly rides point up. Wind the thread to the center of the hook and tie in the Cactus Chenille or Estaz. Wrap the thread back up to the dumbbell, and then wind the Estaz down to the bend of the hook and back up to the dumbbell. This makes a slightly thicker body on the forward part of the crayfish (which is the rear of the hook). Wind the chenille around the dumbbell and tie it off. Cut out the carapace/claws piece. For this, use Bug Skin or cloth-backed vinyl cut into a rectangular shape and then cut halfway through lengthwise to form the two claws. Position the hook with the point up so that the carapace will be on the fly's back. Punch a hole near the end of the carapace, slide it over the hook eye, and secure

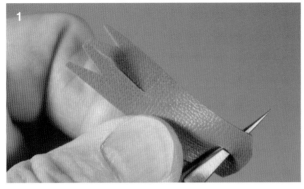

The first step of a simple crayfish pattern is to make a cara-pace of cloth-backed vinyl or similar material. Trim the mate-rial to this shape and punch a hole in the tail end for the hook eye.

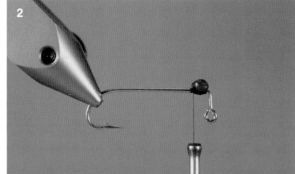

Tie a dumbbell to the bottom of a jig hook.

Make the body of the crayfish with plastic chenille such as Estaz or Cactus Chenille.

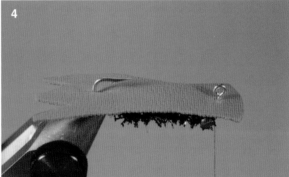

Slip the hole in the carapace over the hook eye and position the carapace over the body and with the claws on the sides of the hook point.

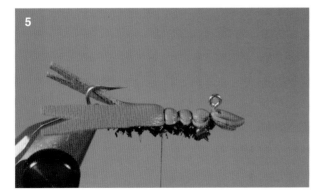

Spiral the thread over the carapace, moving the thread for-ward under the fly and making two wraps every time the thread passed over the carapace.

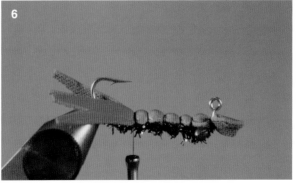

Continue wrapping to bind down the carapace.

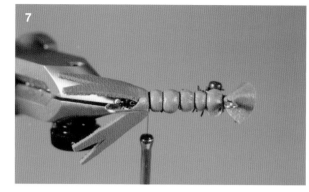

The last band of thread will splay the claws. Whip-finish the thread here.

Plastic chenille with extra-long fibers makes a crayfish body that looks like it has legs.

the material in place with two wraps of thread. Hold the carapace over the back of the fly and spiral-wrap the thread to the bend of the hook. Make several tight wraps at the bend and tie off the thread there. If you like, make V cuts in the ends of the claws.

### HELLGRAMMITES

Hellgrammites are large, black, ugly, bottom-dwelling creatures that provide a good mouthful to large trout and smallmouths. They grow to about 3 inches long. Fly tiers have invented lots of patterns that look like hellgrammites. Most of these patterns are complicated and time consuming, but a good hellgrammite doesn't have to be complex and hard to tie, as the following pattern of my own design demonstrates.

#### Pfeiffer's Simple Hellgrammite

With two materials, you can make a reasonable hellgrammite that will catch a ton of fish. Usually, hellgrammites are pictured straight and flat in books, and imitations are often tied on straight-shank hooks. You can do the same with this pattern, but I also like to tie it on a curved-shank hook so that the fly will resemble the free-drifting hellgrammites that tend to curl or roll up.

**Hook:** Long- or curved-shank hook (such as a Mustad 37160), size 2/0 through 8.
**Thread:** Black.
**Body:** Black Cactus Chenille or Estaz.
**Carapace:** Black material such as Thin Skin, Pleather, Bug Skin, vinyl, or cloth-backed vinyl.

The simple way to make this fly is to tie on at the rear of the hook, then attach the black Cactus Chenille or Estaz and wrap the thread forward. Follow with the chenille. Then cut a rectangular carapace from vinyl or Thin Skin. Trim each end into a fork shape, and then hold the carapace over the body as you spiral-wrap and rib the fly from the head back to the tail. The forks at each end will extend from the fly's body and resemble the antennae.

To tie a simple hellgrammite, first attach a length of Cactus Chenille to a straight hook or a curved hook such as this Mustad 37160.

Wrap the thread forward and then follow it with the Cactus Chenille.

Cut a rectangle of black cloth-backed vinyl for the carapace. Notch the ends to make feelers and tails.

Lay the carapace on top of the body and tie it in place with spiral wraps of thread.

Examples of finished hellgrammite flies. Trout and small-mouths like this pattern.

Whip-finish at the rear. Give the fly a shiny appearance and protect the thread with a coat of head cement over the back. Variations include first sliding a black bead on the hook for weight, adding some lead wire wraps before tying, or adding a single or double mono weedguard for fishing in snaggy water.

### BOTTOM WORMS AND CRAWLERS
#### Pfeiffer's Simple Bass Worm
**Hook:** Long or short shank, size 2/0 through 6.
**Thread:** Black or to match the fly's color.
**Weight:** Dumbbell eyes.
**Tail and body:** Cactus Chenille or Estaz, twisted and tied as a tail and then wrapped around the shank for a body.

This is very similar to the Twisted 'Cuda Fly in chapter 10, except for the material used. For this fly, use Cactus Chenille to make a bulky, wormlike fly that can snake along the bottom. Cut a length of chenille about three times as long as the desired length of the finished fly. That is, if you want a 4-inch fly, start with a piece of Cactus Chenille about 12 inches long. Attach the chenille at the rear of the hook shank, then hold the material about two-thirds along its length and twist it. Make sure that you twist in the same direction as the twist in the Cactus Chenille's core; otherwise the chenille will come apart. Experiment with the number of turns. Fold the twisted part over a bodkin and hold the end of the chenille against the hook shank. Remove the bodkin—when you do, the doubled chenille will twist itself into a spiral—and bind the chenille to the hook. Wind the thread forward, and then wrap the remaining Cactus Chenille around the hook shank to make the body. Tie off at the front of the hook. Variations include adding dumbbell eyes for weight and adding a bushy hackle collar at the head.

Begin a one-material worm fly by tying a piece of Cactus Chenille to the rear of the hook. Twist the material, double it back on itself, and attach it to the hook.

When you let go of the tail, the doubled material will twist into a rope.

Wrap the remaining single strand of Cactus Chenille around the hook to make the worm's head.

Different sizes and styles of plastic chenille let you make a variety of fly-rod worms.

Worm flies usually need some extra weight. A dumbbell works well, but you can also use a bead or metal cone.

Long, thin, and slinky, this simple fly is a fly fisher's equivalent of a Texas-rigged plastic worm.

### Simple Bass Bottom Crawler

This buggy-looking fly can resemble a large nymph, a crayfish, a leech or almost anything else underwater.

**Hook:** Long or short shank, size 2/0 through 6. A jig hook is a good alternative, particularly when fishing in snaggy water.
**Thread:** Black or to match the rest of the fly.
**Weight:** Dumbbell eyes tied to the front of the hook shank and on top so that that the fly will ride point up.
**Tail:** Marabou in any color desired. Popular colors for bass include purple, blue, black, olive green, brown, dark red, and yellow.
**Body:** Palmered, oversize hackle. The body color can match or contrast with the tail.

This fly is a simple version of a large Woolly Bugger, with dumbbell eyes for weight. The marabou makes for a very seductive tail that has lots of movement, even with minimal twitching of the fly. First attach the dumbbell, and then wrap to the rear of the hook shank and tie in the marabou. Leave the butt ends so that you can wrap over them to add bulk to the body. Tie in one or more oversize hackles, then wrap the thread forward and over the marabou butts. Palmer the hackles forward and tie them off at the dumbbell. Whip-finish the thread.

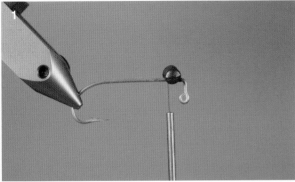

To tie a simple Bottom Crawler, use a jig hook weighted with a metal dumbbell.

Wrap to the rear of the hook and then tie in the marabou tail.

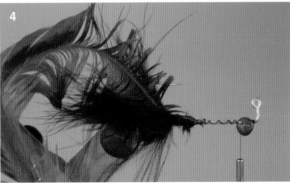

To make an extra-thick tail, add a second tuft of marabou.

Tie in at least one oversize hackle.

Advance the thread and then spiral the hackle forward to complete the body.

# 7

chapter

Terrestrials are those flies that imitate land insects that can end up in the water and become food for fish, particularly trout. Most articles, books, and seminars on terrestrials revolve around trout fishing, though terrestrials are also ideal for pond panfish and sometimes even smallmouths and fallfish. The category includes beetles, ants, termites, grasshoppers, crickets, inchworms, caterpillars, bees, wasps, hornets, ladybugs, cicadas, and similar insects. As simple flies, they rank high in ease of tying. They are also fun to fish.

**INCHWORMS**

Although you will never run across a "hatch" of inchworms, you will see them falling from trees and bushes during the spring and summer. Inchworm imitations should be in the fly box of any trout fisherman. And while there are some complex patterns involving deer hair and such, there are also some simple patterns. One of these is the Green Weenie, a fly popular in the mid-Atlantic area and gaining popularity throughout the country. It is nothing more than an inchworm-like fly of chenille that can be tied weighted or unweighted. Both can be tied with standard chenille, using green or more often a chartreuse shade to get the bright green color that trout seem to like. You can also tie the same fly using a thread base of yellow or bright green over which you tie a wrap of green Larva Lace or similar plastic material. The green base serves as an internal color for the translucent plastic overwrap. A variation of these is a green inchworm on which the chenille is tied at both ends of the hook shank and arched in the middle to resemble an inchworm curling in distress or walking along a twig. A third similar pattern is a green or chartreuse fly of Vernille or Ultra Chenille tied to the hook shank with both tapered ends extending so as to imitate a worm, similar to a San Juan Worm pattern.

Green Weenie
**Hook:** Standard length to 2X long, size 8 through 14.
**Thread:** A shade of green that matches the chenille.
**Body:** Green or chartreuse chenille.

Attach the chenille at the end of the hook shank, then fold over a loop and tie it down to leave a doubled end of chenille. Then wrap the thread to the front of the hook, continue with the chenille, tie off and clip the chenille, and finish the head. Seal with head cement.

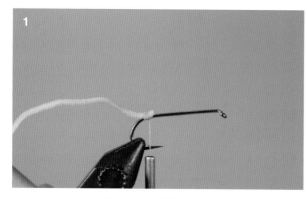

To make a Green Weenie, first tie in a length of chartreuse Ultra Chenille at the rear of the hook.

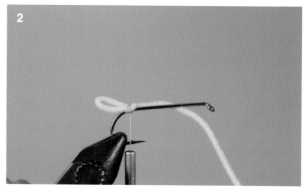

Fold the chenille over to make a short looped tail, and tie it down with the thread.

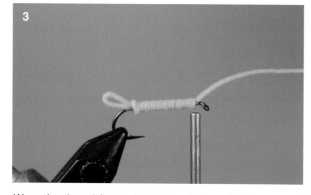

Wrap the thread forward and then follow with the wrap of chenille.

Complete the fly by clipping the excess chenille after tying it off and then finishing the head.

### Larva Lace Green Weenie

**Hook:** Standard length to 2X long, size 8 through 14. A curved-shank nymph hook is ideal.

**Thread:** A shade of green that matches the Larva Lace.

**Body:** Underbody of thread; overbody of green or chartreuse Larva Lace.

Tie in the Larva Lace partway down the bend of the hook. Wrap the green thread evenly to the eye of the hook, and follow it with the Larva Lace. Tie off and clip the Larva Lace, finish the head, and apply head cement.

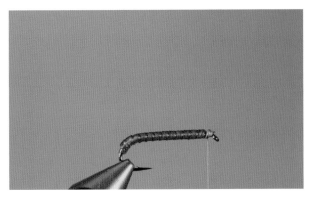

The Larva Lace Green Weenie is another simple, one-material inchworm pattern. It consists of green Larva Lace (a translucent, plastic material) wrapped over a base of green thread.

Walking Inchworm

**Hook:** Standard to 2X long, size 6 through 12.

**Thread:** Black or brown.

**Body:** Green or chartreuse Vernille or Ultra Chenille.

To make a Walking Inchworm, attach the thread at the rear of the hook and then tie in a length of yellow, light green, or chartreuse Ultra Chenille.

Wind the thread forward on the hook shank.

Tie down the Ultra Chenille again, making an arch to simulate a walking inchworm.

Attach the thread at the rear of the hook shank, then tie in the Vernille or Ultra Chenille. Wrap the thread forward to the hook eye, then fold the chenille in a high loop and tie it down. Clip the excess, finish the head, and seal. The black thread blends with the hook to make it look like a stick, while the arch of the chenille resembles the worm.

### Simple Inchworm

**Hook:** Standard to 2X long, size 6 through 12.
**Thread:** Green or chartreuse.
**Body:** Green or chartreuse Vernille or Ultra Chenille.

Attach the thread at the rear of the hook shank, then tie down the chenille, leaving a tag end ½ to 1 inch long. Spiral-wrap over the chenille up to the eye of the hook and tie off, clipping the thread and sealing it with head cement. Leave a forward tag end of about ½ to 1 inch of chenille. Finish by heating the ends of the chenille in a flame and rolling them with your fingers to taper them.

Begin a Simple Inchworm by tying one end of a piece of Ultra Chenille or Vernille atop the hook.

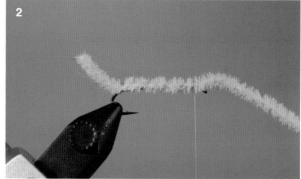

Spiral-wrap the thread over the body to secure the chenille to the hook. Use a thread that matches the chenille.

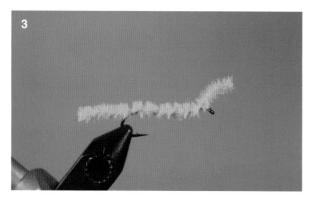

Tie off the thread. Clip the ends of the chenille to length.

## BEETLES

There are about 60,000 beetle species worldwide, and more than 14,000 species in the United States. Many beetles fall into streams and farm ponds where trout and panfish eat them. Beetle imitations fit the concept of simple flies perfectly. A beetle imitation is nothing more than a bulky body with a bunch (six, actually) of stubby legs. You don't have to stick to only six legs, since trout and panfish can't count.

One of the simplest ways to tie beetles is with foam, using thin sheet foam (about ⅛ inch or 2 mm in thickness) available from fly-tying, craft, art, and school-supply stores. The basics of a beetle like this are the legs, tied to the hook shank, and the body, attached at the rear of the hook and folded over. This simple construction makes it easy to tie beetles in a number of styles and with a number of materials, though never more than two materials on any one fly.

### Crowe Beetle

**Hook:** Standard length, size 8 through 20.
**Thread:** Black or to match body color.
**Body:** Deer hair.

Although it's made of deer hair, this fly does not require any spinning or stacking. Tying it is almost as easy as tying a foam beetle. Start by picking the right type of hair. Cow elk is coarse and better suited to large beetles; yearling elk and coastal deer are much finer, and therefore better for small flies.

Clip a bundle of deer hair, comb out the underfur, and tie the butt ends of the hair to the rear of the hook shank. Then wind the thread forward. Fold the bundle of hair over the top of the hook and tie it down. Make sure that you are not tight against the eye; you don't want the trimmed hair to block the hook eye. After tying down the hair with a loose wrap and then tight wraps, whip-finish the thread and seal the wrap. Clip the ends of the deer hair to make the beetle's head. If you want the fly to have legs, pull out a hair or two on each side.

To tie a Crowe beetle, first clean and stack a small bundle of black deer hair. Tie the tips of the hair to the rear of the hook shank.

Wrap the thread forward, and then fold over the deer hair and tie it down to form the body.

Beetles come in different sizes and shapes. If you want a fatter bug (like this one), begin with a thicker clump of hair.

Tie off the thread and clip the hair to make the beetle's head.

These two Crowe Beetles show the variety of flies that can be tied this way.

Although black is the standard color, you can also tie these in brown, gray, green, tan, and other colors to simulate beetles in your fishing area. You can also vary the bulk of the deer hair and adjust the degree of "pull" on the bundle before tying it down to vary the proportions from a fat Japanese beetle or ladybug shape to an elongated click beetle or long-horn beetle shape. For long-body beetles, use 2X- or 3X-long hooks.

### Basic Foam Beetle

**Hook:** Standard length, size 10 through 20.
**Thread:** Black or to match body color.
**Body:** Black sheet foam, or a color to match beetles in your area.
**Legs:** Black or black-sparkle Cactus Chenille.

Secure the thread to the hook shank at the rear, then tie down one point of a football-shaped or teardrop-shaped piece of foam. Tie in a length of Cactus Chenille (regular or medium for sizes 10 to 14, fine for hook sizes 16 through 20). Cactus Chenille or Estaz makes short, buggy legs on beetles like this one. Wind the thread forward, followed by

To tie a Basic Foam Beetle, attach a small, teardrop-shaped piece of foam to the hook. Then tie in a length of Cactus Chenille.

Wrap the Cactus Chenille forward and tie it off. Clip the excess chenille.

Pull the foam over the back of the fly and tie it down behind the hook eye.

The foam makes the carapace and provides flotation. The Cactus Chenille adds a little sparkle and resembles the beetle's legs.

Ladybugs can be tied the same way. Use thin red foam and then add spots with paint or a felt-tip pen.

several turns of the chenille, and then tie off and clip the chenille. Fold the foam body over the hook and secure it with a few loose wraps followed by tight wraps. Tie down the foam just in back of the hook eye. Use one of the very thin foams (0.5 or 1.0 mm) available from fly-tying shops for tying very small beetles.

### Japanese Beetle

**Hook:** Standard length, size 8 through 12.
**Thread:** Black or dark green.
**Body:** Dark green, shiny, flat foam, or foam strips from Bill Skilton Flies, USA.
**Legs:** Copper-colored Cactus Chenille or a similar material.

Japanese beetles, while fortunately (for agriculture) not as abundant as they once were, are still a staple food of trout on some streams, and patterns that imitate them remain effective. Since they are shiny beetles with an iridescence that changes from green to copper depending upon the light, the best foam is one that is shiny with copper and green colors, such as that available from Bill Skilton Flies, USA. The technique of tying is the same as that for a Basic Foam Beetle.

### Floating Ladybug Beetle

**Hook:** Size 14 or 16.
**Thread:** Black.
**Body:** Red closed-cell foam.
**Legs:** Black Cactus Chenille.

This is just a variation of the Basic Foam Beetle. It is tied the same way, but with red foam. Unlike many other beetles, ladybugs are highly beneficial in that they help to control aphids, which are destructive to home gardens. They are bought for this purpose by many serious gardeners.

### Sinking Ladybug Beetle

**Hook:** Size 14 or 16.
**Thread:** Black.
**Body:** Red material such as Pleather, cloth-backed vinyl, opaque red vinyl, or Swiss Straw.
**Legs:** Black Cactus Chenille.

This is tied like the surface beetles, but with non-floating materials so that the fly will sink. Often, the best use of this is as a dropper off a dry fly.

### Coffee Bean Beetle No. 1

Coffee bean beetles are not new. Charlie Fox and Vince Marinaro worked with some in the 1930s, and they might have been old hat by then. They are re-invented now and again by fly tiers who realize that the shape, size, and color of a coffee bean closely resembles many beetles and that a coffee bean added to a hook might be a great fly. It is, but it's not as durable as foam. Coffee beans do float, so there is no problem there.

By slotting a coffee bean with a hacksaw blade, you can turn it into the body of a beetle pattern. Glue the bean to a hook shank after tying legs to the hook. Sealing the bean with head cement or nail polish will keep it from absorbing water.

The main advantage is that you can get huge supply of material with the purchase of an ounce or two of mixed beans from your local food store. Another advantage of a coffee bean is that you only have to slot it and glue it to the hook, adding some legs either before or after the gluing stage.

It is best to seal the coffee bean with head cement to make it a tad more durable when fishing. This also presents a problem; if you seal the bean after tying and get some sealer on rubber legs, you tend to twist, harden, and deform the legs. If you are making bean beetles with rubber or plastic legs and tying them to the hook first, take care with the sealing process or seal the bean first, and then epoxy it to the hook. Or you can make the legs with hackle fibers, dyed-black deer hair, or a black synthetic such as Super Hair, tying the legs onto the middle of the hook shank and then gluing the bean on the hook. These materials will not be affected by the sealer. You can also glue the bean to the hook with some extra room in back of the eye, seal the bean, and, after the sealer has dried, attach the legs in front of the bean.

**Hook:** Standard length to 2X long, size 8 through 12.
**Thread:** Black.
**Body:** Coffee bean.
**Legs:** Rubber, silicone, or plastic legs.

Pick a coffee bean that is undamaged and evenly ovalar in shape, and slot it along the long axis with a hacksaw blade. Attach the thread at the center of the hook, and then tie on the legs. Tie off the thread and trim the legs as desired (this can also be done after completing the beetle). Apply some mixed epoxy to the slot in the bean and to the hook shank, and add the bean to the hook. Remove the beetle from the vise and place it point up (upside down) on your workbench to cure. Glue a bunch at a time and check frequently to make sure that each hook stays at right angles to the beetle body as the glue cures. After the epoxy has cured, pull the legs away from the body and seal the bean with head cement or clear nail polish.

Coffee Bean Beetle No. 2

**Hook:** 2X long, size 8 through 12.

**Thread:** Black.

**Body:** Coffee bean.

**Legs:** Hackle, deer hair, synthetic hair, or any rubber or plastic leg material.

Choose a bean as above, matching the bean to the hook size. Spiral-wrap the thread up and down the hook for better gluing, and secure the thread with half hitches in back of the hook eye. Cut the thread at least a foot away from the fly; you will use the thread hanging from the front of the hook to attach the legs. Slot the bean with a hacksaw blade, then epoxy it onto the hook. Make sure that you leave about ⅛ of an inch of space in back of the eye for tying on the legs. Remove the hook from the vise and turn it over. Let the epoxy cure, and then seal the bean with head cement. Let the sealer dry, replace the hook in the vise, and using the tag end of thread, tie in the legs. Finish the head and seal it with cement.

To use hackle for the legs, simply tie on and wrap the feather just as you would on a dry or wet fly. Then trim the ends of the fibers and clip the top and bottom of the collar to make legs sticking out from the beetle. Heavy, webby black hackle is best for this.

Deer hair, synthetics, and rubber leg material can be added by tying the material in place on the hook shank and then spreading it sideways, or seating the material by folding it over the tying thread, pulling it to the hook shank on each side, and then tying off.

Jassid

This is a term for a basic beetle-like fly (also described as a leafhopper, but without the "tent" wings of those insects) developed by the Marinaro/Fox team. It is easy to tie and can resemble a number of beetles and beetle-like insects.

Jassids, popularized more than 50 years ago, are still good flies. A jassid is simple, too, consisting of only a wrap of hackle and a jungle-cock feather that represents the back of the insect.

**Hook:** Standard length, size 12 through 20.
**Thread:** Black.
**Hackle:** Black.
**Back:** Jungle-cock nail (or another flat feather trimmed to shape and lacquered).

This is designed to imitate leafhoppers. Wrap the hackle first, trimming it on the top and cutting a V underneath the hook. Then tie a jungle-cock nail flat on top. If you don't have jungle cock, you can use any small, dense feather trimmed and lacquered to make it hard like the natural nail of the jungle cock.

## ANTS

The 15,000 species of ants found in North America range from about 2 to 13 mm in length and from black to cinnamon in color. They all have similar shapes, with well-defined heads, thoraxes, and abdomens. Ant patterns are relatively easy to tie using any of several basic methods. One of the most popular contemporary methods is the McMurray style, in which the head/thorax and abdomen are separate pieces glued on monofilament. The mono is attached to the center of the hook shank and then covered with a wrap of hackle that simulates legs. The original pattern required threading thin cylinders of balsa onto a length of mono and then painting them black. But there are some simpler ways to make ants.

### Foam McMurray Ant

**Hook:** Standard length, size 8 through 18.
**Thread:** To match the color of the body.
**Body:** Small strip of foam cut from sheet foam or a tiny foam cylinder. The piece should be about as thick as a matchstick (or slightly larger or smaller, depending upon hook size). For very small flies, use the very thin foams available from fly shops in 0.5 and 1 mm thicknesses.
**Hackle:** To match the color of the body, trimmed on the bottom to let the ant float low in the surface film.

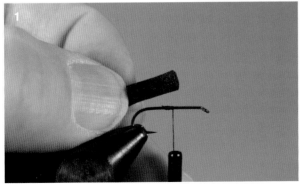

To tie a Foam McMurray Ant, first prepare or cut a foam cylinder or rectangle. Attach the thread to center of the hook shank.

Tie down the piece of closed-cell foam. Wrap enough thread to create the ant's waist.

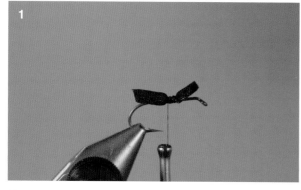

You can also make foam ants from sheet foam cut into small rectangles and tied in place. From the fish's perspective, the fly has an accurate silhouette.

Complete the Foam McMurray Ant by adding a wrap of black hackle.

The wrap of hackle represents the ant's legs; the foam provides buoyancy.

The secret of tying this fly is to use thread heavy enough to tightly wrap the foam to the shank in the center of the hook so as to make a thin and distinct waist in the fly. Lacking that, you can tie on one piece of foam pointed to the rear for the abdomen and a second shorter length pointed forward for the head and abdomen, though this does make the fly more complicated. To finish the fly, wrap the center with a hackle and trim the hackle close along the belly so that the fly floats low and lifelike. In smaller sizes, you can dispense with the hackle and just use the body.

## Underwater Ant

**Hook:** Standard length, size 10 through 16.
**Thread:** To match the body color.
**Body:** Fine EZ-Dub for larger sizes, Lagartun Spun Fur for small sizes. Good colors are black, brown, cinnamon, and red.
**Legs:** Hackle the same color as the body.

This fly is easy to tie, since you are just making two balls or bundles of body material to make the abdomen and the thorax/head parts. First make the rear or abdomen bundle, then wrap over the strand of body material with the working thread to make a long waist before wrapping the material to make the thorax and head. Make the waist longer than you think necessary, since some of the thorax/head material will build up farther to the rear than planned. Tie off and clip the excess body material. Then tie in the hackle at the waist area, wind a few turns, and tie off the feather. Whip-finish the thread and clip it. Alternatively, you can tie the abdomen, then the hackle, then the head.

To tie a Cinnamon Underwater Ant, first tie in a length of yarn or material such as the EZ-Dub shown here.

Wrap the body material around the hook shank and tie it off in the middle of the hook.

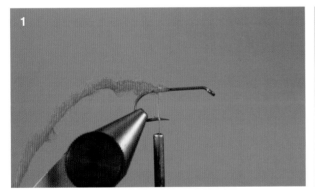

Attach a hackle in front of the abdomen.

Make a few wraps with the hackle.

Wind the thread forward and then wrap the rest of the body material to form the thorax and head.

Because the body material is absorbent, this ant will soak up some water and sink.

### Carpenter Ant

**Hook:** 2X long, size 8 or 10.
**Thread:** Black or to match the body color.
**Body:** A strip or tiny cylinder of black, cinnamon, red, or brown closed-cell foam.
**Legs:** Deer hair the same color as the body.

The main difference between this fly and other ant patterns is that this one is a longer, larger imitation tied to have three separate segments of abdomen, thorax, and head. The foam body keeps it in the surface film and the deer hair legs make it look natural. Secure the thread just aft of the middle of the hook shank, and tie down the rear half of the foam body. Then wrap the thread forward and tie the foam down again to separate the thorax and head. Finish by attaching a few fibers of deer hair on each side, then tie off with a whip finish. Clip the deer hair to leg length.

### TERMITES

There are fewer species of termites than of most other terrestrials, but you still might want a few imitations in your box. Basically, tying these is nothing more than tying bigger, white ants, using the same techniques as for those patterns.

### Foam Termite

**Hook:** 2X long, size 8 through 12.
**Thread:** White.
**Body:** White closed-cell foam, either a piece cut from sheet foam or a thin cylinder.
**Hackle:** White.

Tie this like a McMurray Foam Ant, but make a longer abdomen to correspond to the longer abdomen of the real insect. The rest of the tying is just like the ants above. You can also tie this fly using some of the white cricket or bug preformed foam bodies sold at all fly shops.

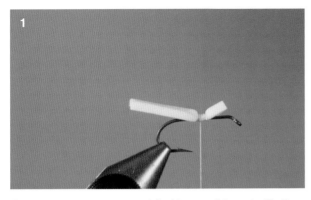

Termite patterns are essentially bigger, white ants. To tie a Foam Termite, prepare a piece of white foam long enough to simulate the abdomen. Tie the foam to the hook.

Add a white hackle to make the fly's legs.

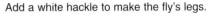

### Underwater Termite
**Hook:** 2X long, size 8 through 12.
**Thread:** White.
**Body:** White yarn, fine chenille, EZ-Dub, or a similar material.
**Hackle:** White.

Tie this with the same technique used for underwater ants. Secure the thread at the rear of the hook shank, tie in the body material, and wrap the thread forward to the midpoint of the hook. Wrap the abdomen, and then wrap over the body material for ⅛ of an inch to form a waist. Finish by wrapping the head/abdomen, tying it off at the waist. Then attach a hackle, make a few wraps, and whip-finish.

### Twisted-Tail Termite
**Hook:** Standard length, size 8 through 12.
**Thread:** White.
**Body:** White yarn, EZ-Dub, or a similar material.
**Hackle:** White.

This is a slightly different tie. Attach the thread at the center of the hook shank, and then tie in a length of body material. Instead of wrapping the body around the hook shank, twist the end in the same direction as the natural lay. Double a short length of the twisted material over a bodkin, and bind the strand to the hook shank. When you remove the bodkin, the doubled material will twist into a tight body. Attach and wrap a hackle, tie off the feather, and then continue to wrap the body material forward to make a head. Whip-finish the thread. If you use a water-resistant body material, this fly will float; if you use a water-absorbent material, it will sink.

Make a body for a Twisted-Tail Termite by furling (twisting) a piece of white yarn or similar material. The method is just like that for the Simple Bass Worm in chapter 6.

Add a wrap of white hackle in front of the abdomen.

Finish the fly with a turn or two of the body material to make the thorax and head.

### GRASSHOPPERS

Various sizes and colors of grasshoppers are found throughout the country. In early spring, most are small and light green, while hoppers found in late summer and early fall are larger and mottled brown. They are typically found in meadows and similar habitats. Grasshopper imitations are very good flies for big trout and farm-pond panfish and bass. Since they are relatively large flies, hoppers often require slightly heavier gear than the 3- and 4-weight outfits that are ideal for ants, jassids, small beetles, and such.

Foam Hopper

**Hook:** 3X long, size 4 through 8.
**Thread:** Light green or to match the body color.
**Body:** A green to mottled brown foam cylinder.
**Wing:** A bundle of turkey fibers tied down over the foam body.

Use light tan or light green foam to make a grasshopper body that you can cover with a wing material. The foam will ensure that the hopper will float.

Cover the foam body with a layer or two of turkey fibers to simulate the wings of a hopper.

Secure the thread about a third of the shank length in back of the hook eye, and then tie down the foam body. The body should be about one-and-a-quarter times the length of the hook shank. When you attach the body to the hook, the front of the foam cylinder should be just behind the hook eye. Then tie in a bundle of turkey fibers for a wing, securing them in place over the foam tie-down point. Trim the excess turkey and whip-finish the thread. You can tie these simple hoppers in light green (for spring and early summer) and mottled brown (for late summer and fall) and in sizes to suit your fishing.

Poly-Yarn Hopper

**Hook:** 3X or 4X long, size 4 through 8.
**Thread:** Green or brown.
**Body:** Twisted poly yarn in colors from light green through medium brown.
**Wing:** A bundle of deer hair, secured in one spot and tied down like a Muddler Minnow wing.

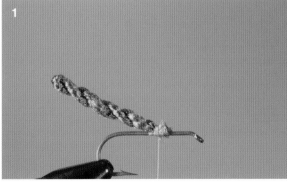

To make a Poly-Yarn Hopper, use green or tan polypropylene yarn and furl (twist) it to form a body.

Finish the fly by adding a bundle of tan deer hair to form the wing and help the hopper float.

This fly uses the furling technique of twisting the body yarn after tying one end to the hook about one-third of the shank length behind the eye. Twist in same direction as the manufacturer's twist. Fold the twisted yarn over a bodkin, secure the other end to the hook, and remove the bodkin to allow the yarn to twist into a rope. Clip any excess yarn. Then attach a bundle of clipped, combed, and stacked deer hair, tying it down so that the clipped butt ends will serve as a head, much as they do on a Muddler Minnow. The water-resistant poly yarn and the hollow deer hair will help keep this fly afloat.

Fall Cork Hopper
**Hook:** 2X or 3X long, size 4 through 8.
**Thread:** Tan.
**Body:** Unpainted cork cylinder, no larger in diameter than the hook gap, tapered on two sides at the back.
**Wing:** Deer hair, trimmed on the bottom to resemble legs.

This is a simple tie, since it does not involve painting the cork, which is already about the same color as autumn grasshoppers. By veiling the deer hair around the front of the cork body, you can push some fibers around to the belly, where they can be clipped to form a semblance of grasshopper legs. Trim the butts to make the head like that of a Muddler Minnow. Cork cylinders are easy to taper into the tent-like shape of the rear wings of a grasshopper.

Make a Fall Cork Hopper by tying and gluing a tapered cork body to the hook and then covering it with a bundle of deer hair.

## CRICKETS

There are three main types of crickets: field (black), camel, and mole (both brown). Of these, the large black cricket is the most common, typically found in woods and meadow areas. You can fish cricket imitations for trout, panfish, largemouth bass, smallmouth bass, and anything else that takes food off the surface. Imitations of these insects are similar to those of grasshoppers; only the colors differ for most simple patterns.

Foam Cricket

**Hook:** 3X long, size 6 through 10.
**Thread:** Black.
**Body:** Black foam.
**Wing:** Dyed-black turkey or duck quill (if long enough) or black deer hair.

Tie this the same way as the Foam Hopper, attaching the foam body to the hook shank and then covering it with a bundle of black deer hair or dyed turkey quill. To switch to the brown cricket imitations (mole and camel), just tie it with dark brown materials.

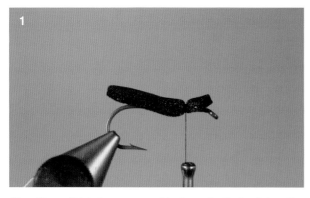

Tie a Foam Cricket as you would a foam-bodied ant, termite, or hopper. Attach a long piece of foam that will simulate the cricket's body.

Tie in a section of dyed-black or brown turkey feather over the foam to simulate the back and legs of the cricket.

Another type of simple cricket has a furled or twisted body of heavy yarn or EZ-Dub covered with black deer hair that represents legs.

Cylinders (left) and sheet foam both work on simple cricket patterns.

Yarn Underwater Cricket

**Hook:** 2X long, size 6 through 10.
**Thread:** Black.
**Body:** Black yarn.
**Wing:** Black bear hair or black duck quill (primarily for smaller hooks).

Tie this just as you would a Poly-Yarn Hopper, furling the yarn to make a twisted body that is about the length of the hook shank, then adding a wing of hair or wing-quill fibers. By using knitting yarn (as opposed to polypropylene yarn), you will make a pattern that sinks. Use brown materials to make mole and camel cricket imitations.

## BEES, WASPS, AND HORNETS

Various species of bees, wasps, and hornets live throughout North America. They range in size from the tiny bees often know as sweat bees (they don't sting, but like to light on you to drink your sweat) to the giant cicada killers, which do not generally bother people, but are as large as cigar butts. They have to be, since they catch large cicadas on the wing, and then stuff the paralyzed insects into their burrows for their larvae to feed on. Flies that resemble bees and wasps will catch a variety of fish.

Surface Bee

**Hook:** Size 6 through 10 humped-shank hook.
**Thread:** Black.
**Body:** Yellow foam cylinder or bug body colored with black bands and threaded onto the hook.
**Wings:** Brown hackle.

This is more like a surface bug, but without the tail of a typical popper. Use a foam cylinder no larger in diameter than the gap of the hook. Color the cylinder with thin black bands, using a permanent felt-tip marker. Then cut the cylinder to about two-thirds of the

To make a Surface Bee, tie down a yellow cylinder of foam and then band the foam with a black felt-tip marker.

hook-shank length. Make a pilot hole along one side of the body, and thread the hook into the bug body, using CA glue to secure it. Then attach the thread, tie in a brown hackle, wrap the hackle, and tie it off. The result is a good-looking bee pattern that works well, particularly when fished with tiny twitches that will simulate the buzzing and movement of a bee on the surface.

### Underwater Bee
**Hook:** Size 6 through 12.
**Thread:** Black.
**Body:** Yellow and black chenille.
**Hackle:** Brown.

Although this fly has three materials, it is as easy to tie as a simple wet fly with a body and hackle. Attach the thread to the rear of the hook shank, and then tie in (together or separately) lengths of black and yellow chenille. At this point, there are two ways to tie the fly. One is to hold the two colors of chenille together and wrap them forward, then tie

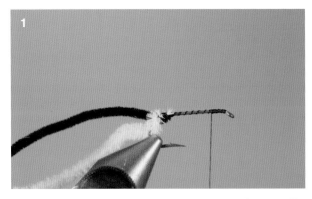

To tie an Underwater Bee, attach black and yellow chenille at the rear of the hook shank. Then wrap the thread forward to just behind the hook eye.

Wrap the two materials forward and tie them off with the thread.

Complete the bee with a collar-style brown or white hackle.

them off at about one-fourth of the shank length in back of the hook eye. The other way is to twist the two lengths of chenille together and then wrap this double strand up the hook shank and tie it off. The first method will give you a banded effect, while the second will give you more of a mottled, mixed effect. The fish won't care. After tying off the chenille and clipping the excess, tie in and wrap a brown hackle, tie off and clip the excess feather, and whip-finish the thread. To get down deep, you can tie this bee with weight, such as a metal cone or bead, a length of lead wire, or a wrap of wire on the hook shank.

### Floating Wasp/Hornet
**Hook:** 2X long, size 4 through 8.
**Thread:** Black.
**Body:** Black foam cylinder or bug body (for small hooks) colored with felt-tip markers. The body should be about three-quarters the length of the hook.
**Wings:** White hackle or white Unique (a synthetic wing material).

Tie this as you would any surface bug. Secure the thread to the center of the hook shank, and tie down the bug body at one end so that it extends out the back of the fly. Wrap forward to make a thin waist, then wrap a built-up ball of thread to form the head of the insect. Make the waist long and thin, since this is a characteristic of wasps and hornets. Attach a hackle between the head and body, wrap and tie it off, trim the excess, and tie off the thread. An alternative is to tie down a small bundle of white Unique or similar fine-denier synthetic, and then veil and splay it around the hook to make it resemble the wings of a wasp or hornet.

### Underwater Yarn Wasp/Hornet
**Hook:** 3X long, size 4 through 8.
**Thread:** Black.
**Body:** Black wool, yarn, or EZ-Dub.
**Wings:** Sparse white Unique or flash material.

Tie this like other underwater flies. Attach the thread at the rear of the hook shank, and tie in the body material. Wrap the thread two-thirds of the shank length forward. Make a bulky body; you might have to wrap several layers of material. Secure the body material, but do not clip the excess. Wrap over the body material for a half-dozen turns to make a thin waist. Lift the body material out of the way, and then wrap the thread only to the head of the fly. Now wrap the body material to make the thorax and head. Tie off and clip the body material. Add sparse wings of Unique or fine flash material. Since some wasps and hornets are a mix of yellow and black, you can also tie this with yellow materials and then touch a black permanent marker to those areas you want black.

## CATERPILLARS
Caterpillars are the larval stage of butterflies and moths, and they sometimes fall into the water and end up as fish food. They seldom escape the notice of fish, since they are sizeable morsels. You can tie complicated caterpillars, but simple flies work just as well.

You don't need to know which of the 20 species of swallowtails or hundreds of other caterpillar species the fish are feeding on; you only have to notice the colors and sizes of the caterpillars prevalent in your area. Most caterpillars are tan, brown, yellowish, light green, or dark green. Some have hairy projections all over their bodies, others have hairs only on one end, some have tufts of hairs extending from both sides, and some few have no hairs at all. The easiest way to make a floating caterpillar imitation is to use foam cylinders wrapped or palmered with a long hackle that is then trimmed for effect.

### Floating Foam Caterpillar

**Hook:** 3X or 4X long, size 2 through 10.
**Thread:** To match the body.
**Body:** A tan, brown, yellow, or green foam cylinder.
**Hackle:** A long saddle hackle. Brown, black, and white are good colors.

The diameter of the foam cylinder should be no greater than the gap of the hook. Make a hole in the foam with a bodkin and then thread the foam onto the hook, gluing it in place with CA glue. Attach the thread at the rear of the hook and tie in a saddle hackle by the tip end. Whip-finish and clip the thread. Tie on again in front of the foam, and then spiral-wrap (palmer) the hackle forward over the foam. Secure the hackle at the head of the fly. Clip the excess, whip-finish, cut the thread, and seal the head.

A variation is to thread the foam onto the hook, tie in the hackle at the head of the fly, and then spiral-wrap the hackle down and back up the body. Use widely spaced spirals, since the double wrap of hackle will make for more hairs.

Another variation is to tie in a hackle at the rear of a bare hook. Then attach a thin strip of foam. Wind the thread forward, and make the body by wrapping the foam strip around the hook. Tie off the foam at the front of the hook. Palmer the hackle over the foam body and finish the fly.

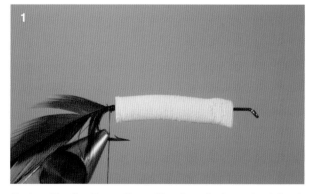

To tie a Floating Foam Caterpillar, thread a long-shank hook (such as a streamer hook) into a foam cylinder. Tie on a hackle at the rear of the hook, and then whip-finish and clip the thread.

Attach the thread at the front of the fly. Palmer the hackle forward and tie it off at the head of the fly. You can clip the hackle to make it more like the short projections and legs of a real caterpillar.

Sinking Caterpillar

**Hook:** 3X or 4X long, size 2 through 10.

**Thread:** Black or red.

**Body:** Standard chenille in yellow, red, black, gray, light green, dark green, or any other color that matches the caterpillars in your area. Match the size of the chenille to the hook size and the bulk of the caterpillar being imitated.

**Hackle:** Black, dark green, gray, brown, white, or yellow saddle hackle palmered over the chenille body. The hackle can be left long or clipped short to more closely resemble the short, spiky tufts of some caterpillars.

You can tie these with bulky bodies or thin bodies, depending upon the type of caterpillar being imitated. The caterpillars of some butterflies (the widespread swallowtails, for instance) and many larger moths are large insects with light green color schemes and few or no spikes or tufts. Those of smaller butterflies and moths are thinner and shorter, and often have lots of tufts sprouting from their bodies. These tufts of hair can grow along the entire body, along the sides, or only at the ends of the caterpillar. Tie and trim accordingly. Omit the palmered saddle hackle on a large caterpillar imitation, but build up the plump body with several back-and-forth wraps of chenille.

To tie a Sinking Caterpillar, wrap a long-hook shank with chenille and then palmer one or more hackles over the body. Clip the hackle fibers short.

With several colors of chenille and a few colors of hackle, you can make imitations of whatever caterpillars live in your part of the country.

chapter

## BASIC POPPERS AND SLIDERS

Surface bugs are often thought of as bass bugs, but that label does not do them justice. Although poppers and sliders are certainly effective for largemouth and smallmouth bass, they also take panfish, perch, pike, pickerel, muskies, striped bass, bluefish, seatrout, redfish, snook, ladyfish, snappers, and a host of other species in both fresh and salt water. In sufficiently large sizes, simple topwater bugs will even catch big-game species such as marlin, sailfish, and sharks. As the following examples show, a fly tier can make a variety of surface bugs without exceeding our three-material limit.

### Potomac River Popper

Lefty Kreh developed his simple Potomac River Popper many years ago, using a small, tapered bottle cork cut at a slant on one end and cut along one side to make a flat belly. Lefty tied it with a tail of squirrel tail, though he has since modified it with a wrap of Cactus Chenille around the hook shank between the tail and the body. You can tie an even simpler variation of the Potomac River Popper that is not painted and does not have a collar.

Sometimes you can find balsa "rods" of the right diameters in hobby shops. These allow you to cut the balsa into short lengths—like slicing a sausage—to make "blanks" for this bug. Unpainted balsa will give you a white or cream bug; natural cork provides a tan or brown bug. These bugs can be made in any size for anything from panfish to big bass and pike.

**Hook:** Long-shank, kinked popper hook, size 2/0 through 14.
**Thread:** Any color. Use finer thread on small hooks, heavier thread on larger hooks.
**Tail:** Squirrel tail is Lefty Kreh's choice, but you can use bucktail, calf tail (for small bugs), synthetic materials, or marabou.
**Body:** Bottle cork or balsa cylinder. The diameter of the body should equal the hook gap. You can also use bullet-shaped corks available from fly shops and catalog houses.

Attach the thread and spiral it up and down the hook shank ahead of the kink to provide added "tooth" for gluing on the body. Then tie on the tail material, making sure that it is in back of the space that the body will occupy. Tie off the thread, but do not seal it. Cut one side of the cork to make a flat belly, and cut the front at a slight angle to make the face of the bug. Slot the cork with a hacksaw blade, mix a puddle of epoxy, and glue the thread-wrapped hook into the slot in the body. Allow the glue to cure. An alternative is to glue the cork to the hook first, then tie in the tail.

If you don't mind adding an extra step, you can dip the body into paint, submerging it so that the paint coats and seals the cork (or balsa). If you use marabou or another fluffy material for the tail, moisten it before painting the body so that it will stand up stiff and not wave around to touch the wet paint. Another variation is to use a round tapered bottle cork, without cutting off one side to make a flat bottom.

To make a simple, unpainted cork bug, cut one side of a bottle cork to make a flat belly, and then use a hacksaw blade to slot the belly of the cork.

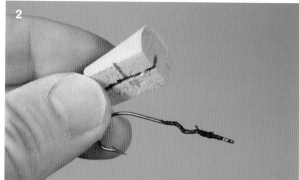

Here's what the shaped and slotted cork looks like. Wrap the hook shank with thread to make for a better glue bond.

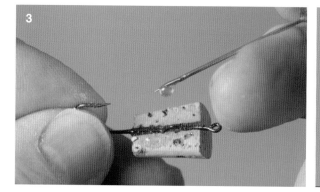

Apply epoxy glue to the wrapped hook shank and to the slot in the cork body. Press the cork onto the hook.

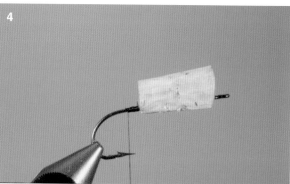

Let the glue cure. Clamp the hook in your vise and attach the thread. Don't worry about leaving the cork unpainted—the fish do not seem to care.

Tie on a tail. You can use squirrel tail, calf tail, synthetic hair, or bucktail.

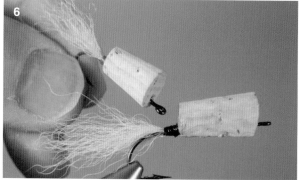

These are about as simple as popping bugs can be, but they work well for bass and other fish.

### Basic Cork/Balsa Slider

Follow the same procedure to make a simple cork slider, using a bottle cork or balsa cylinder that you tapered at the front with a razor blade or fine saw. You can also use a bullet-shaped cork (available from fly shops and catalogs) mounted with the narrow end forward. The construction steps are the same as those for the Potomac River Popper. Experiment with different tail materials, various tail lengths, and different colors of paints.

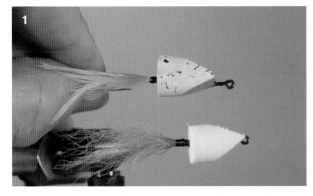

You can make a simple foam or cork slider by cutting the front of a cylinder into a V like the prow of a ship so that it will slide through the water without popping.

You can use natural hair, synthetic materials, or hackle feathers for the tails of sliders. The shape of these flies make them easy to cast.

### Basic Foam Popper

Foam bodies are even easier to use than cork or balsa. Fly shops and catalog houses sell a variety of foam popper bodies and foam cylinders from which bodies can be cut. You can also use the soft closed-cell foam from hair rollers. These hair rollers come in various diameters and different basic colors, each made with a twistable wire that runs through the center of the foam to allow it to hold onto hair.

**Hook:** Long-shank popper hook, size 2/0 through 10.
**Thread:** Any. Use red thread if the wrap securing the tail will show after the body is glued to the hook.
**Tail:** Calf tail, bucktail, squirrel tail, marabou, or synthetic hair.
**Body:** A cylinder of closed-cell foam, a piece cut from an Ethafoam hair roller, or a tapered and shaped foam bug body.

Foam cylinders usually have to be cut to length, while preshaped bug bodies are ready to be glued to hooks. The main difference between harder foam and the softer foam from hair rollers is the type of glue that you use. Otherwise, the construction is the same. First spiral-wrap thread along the hook shank. Then tie in the tail material, after first determining the right spot by measuring the foam body against the hook shank. Tie off with a whip finish and clip the excess thread. Prepare the foam body not by slotting it, but by running a bodkin through the cylinder close to the skin of the belly. Apply glue to the

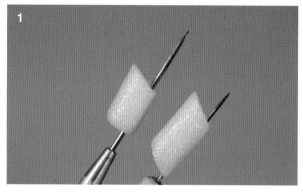

You can use pieces cut from Ethafoam hair rollers to make poppers. Make the pilot hole for the hook close to the belly to preserve hook gap.

First, tie the tail of the bug on the hook, and then use epoxy to glue the Ethafoam body onto the hook.

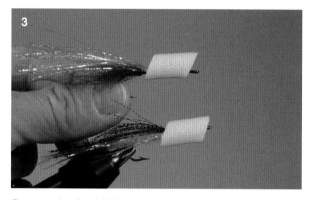

Bugs made of soft Ethafoam aren't as tough as those made of denser, harder foams, but they're easy and inexpensive to make.

hook and slide the body into place. For the firmer closed-cell foams, use CA (cyano-acrylate) glue, applying it to the hook and quickly sliding the hook into the body. Make sure that the body is properly aligned as you slide it onto the hook; CA glue grabs very quickly. For softer (hair-roller) foam, use epoxy, well-mixed and smeared onto the hook shank.

Bodies made from Ethafoam hair rollers work fine, but they're not as tough as harder, denser closed-cell foams. If you want to try hair-roller foam, use wire cutters (wear safety glasses) to cut and remove the wire that runs through the center of each roller. Then cut the hair roller into appropriate lengths for the hooks you're using. As with cork and balsa, the body's diameter should be roughly equal to the hook gap. Once you are sure that the body will slide over the hook from the eye end, add glue and slide the body in place.

You can also make bug bodies out of backer rods used in construction work. Backer rods are available in diameters from ¼ inch to much bigger than you could possibly want for fly tying. These Ethafoam rods can provide a lot of material for surface bugs, but they usually come in only one color: gray.

### Basic Foam Slider

You can make a foam bug into a slider just by cutting one end of the foam at an angle and placing this angle, slope down, at the front of the bug so that it will "wake" rather than pop during the retrieve. One slight problem with this style is that the downward slope of the face may cause the bug to dig into the water when you pick up the line, making casting difficult or jerky. A simple solution is to angle the front of the body on both sides, like the prow of a ship, so that the bug will not dig in on pickup and will still "wake" during a slow retrieve, as a good slider should. The materials and the rest of the construction are the same as the popper's; the only difference is that you cut two angles on the front of the foam body before gluing it to the hook. To make a lot of poppers or sliders, use an assembly-line method. Attach tails to a bunch of hooks and then glue the bodies to the hooks, or glue the bodies first and then add the tails after the glue has cured.

### Bob's Banger

This design by Bob Popovics is a simple tie that allows for interchangeable bodies. You can dress hooks with a variety of tails, prepare bodies in various colors, and then com-

Make a Bob's Banger by tying the tail to the hook and then punching a hole in a foam cylinder. Slide, but don't glue, the body onto the hook. On the water, you can change bodies as you wish.

The lump produced by tying the tail to the hook acts as a stop for the body of a simplified Bob's Banger.

The beauty of the Bob's Banger design is that it lets you combine bodies and tails in the field. This approach reduces the number of flies you need to carry, but it still gives you many color combinations.

bine dressed hooks and bodies in the field to make poppers on the spot. Bob originally designed his Banger for saltwater fishing, but this fly works equally well for freshwater bass and other gamefish that strike on the surface. The original version has a collar of Estaz (a plastic chenille) and a wrap of reflective Mylar tape on the body. This simplified model appeals to a variety of gamefish.

**Hook:** Long shank, size 2/0 through 6.
**Thread:** Heavy rod-wrapping thread; any color.
**Tail:** Any color of bucktail, stacked so that the tips are even. Popular colors include white, yellow, black, red, light green, and orange.
**Body:** A foam cylinder with a hole through the center made with an awl or bodkin.

Tie on at the rear of the hook shank, wrap the thread neatly forward and then back down the hook shank, and tie in a clump of stacked bucktail. Tie off and clip the thread. Use an awl or bodkin to run a hole through the center of a foam body that has been cut to length to fit the hook. Don't glue the body to the hook. Carry the dressed hooks and bodies in separate fly-box compartments, and then match tails and bodies as you please while fishing. Just slide a body onto a dressed hook, tie the hook to your leader, and cast. Mix and match tails and bodies until the fish let you know what they want.

Variations include wrapping a collar of Estaz around the hook shank over the tail wrap, adding a wrap of metallic tape around the foam body, mixing several colors of bucktail, and adding Flashabou or Krystal Flash to the tail. With the Estaz collar and tape-wrapped body, you will have a copy of the original Bob's Banger.

### SANDWICH BUGS

This bug design, which I developed several years ago, consists of the tail or legs glued between two pieces of foam cut from a sheet. The body forms a sandwich, with the hook and tail wrap in the middle. The first step is to develop a body shape that you want, and then cut the backs and bellies of a number of bodies from sheets of foam. Tie a simple tail to a hook, and then glue the top and bottom halves of the body to the hook and each other. You can use bucktail, calf tail, squirrel tail, synthetic hair, saddle hackles, or marabou for the tail.

I've tried various methods to make the foam sandwiches, including CA glue, spray adhesive such as 3M 777, contact glues (such as Weldwood, used to glue laminates to kitchen counters), epoxy, and soft glues such as Pliobond and 3M Ultra Flex. The CA glues can attach your fingers to the bug if you're not careful (which takes some of the fun out of tying simple bugs), and the spray adhesives spray over too wide an area to be functional. The best glues are 3M Ultra Flex and Weldwood contact cement. To use these, tie the tail (or leg) materials to the hook, tie off the thread, and then dab a little glue on the inside surfaces of the pieces of foam. Position the two halves of the body on the hook. Hold the pieces with clamps until the glue cures. Clothespins make good gluing clamps; doll-size clothespins are even better.

The most efficient way to make Sandwich Bugs is to cut out a bunch of body pieces, tie tail materials to a bunch of hooks, and then glue the pieces together. Assembly-line tying is faster than making these bugs one at a time.

You can make Sandwich Bugs in a variety of styles. The following ideas will get you started.

**Hook:** Long-shank, size 2/0 through 6.
**Thread:** Any color.
**Tail:** Four to six saddle hackles. The best colors are white, light green, yellow, black, and tan.
**Body:** Arrowhead-shaped pieces of ⅛-inch or 2 mm foam, in colors to match or contrast with the tail.

Cut the body pieces in advance, making both the same shape and size. Tie on the saddle hackles with all of the feathers nested so that they curve down. This allows the finished bug to resemble a minnow with a damaged swim bladder lying on its side on the surface. Dab a little glue on the top and bottom of the tie-down wraps for the feathers and on the mating parts of the foam. Sandwich the pieces together and clamp them until the glue cures.

Sandwich Minnows, a design of the author's, are made by sandwiching a tail of saddle hackles between two (top and bottom) pieces of sheet foam.

To make a Sandwich Minnow, fold sheet foam and cut it into an arrowhead shape. Punch a hole between the two arrowheads so that you can thread the foam onto a hook shank.

Attach several saddle hackles so that they all curve down. Do not splay them. Then position the foam body in place and add glue to the inside surfaces of the foam and the front of the feathers.

With the glue tacky (or ready to stick, in the case of contact cement), fold the foam to make a flat body like this. If necessary, clamp the body parts with clothespins.

Top view of a completed Sandwich Minnow. This fast, easy fly appeals to a variety of gamefish.

Make a popper or frog the same way, tying down the tail or legs and then gluing body parts to the hook shank. Here, thicker green foam has been used for the top and a thin yellow foam used for the bottom or belly.

Good colors for these flies include all white, all yellow, all light green, all black, red head and white tails, black head and white tails, red head and yellow tails, and green head with yellow tails. If you plan to fish in weeds, add a two-part mono weedguard. Even with a weed guard, this is still a three-material fly.

### Sandwich Frog

**Hook:** Long-shank popper hook, size 2/0 through 6.

**Thread:** Any color.

**Legs:** A bundle of hair attached far enough forward on the hook so that it can be divided into two clumps and glued in position between the body pieces. Good leg materials include stacked bucktail and synthetic hairs; try white, light green, yellow, and black (for night fishing).

**Body:** Ovular- or D-shaped pieces of 2 mm or ⅛-inch foam. Good colors include white, light green, yellow, and black. Although the fish won't care, you can make the top light green and the bottom white, tan, or yellow to more closely match a real frog's colors.

Build this fly the same way as the Sandwich Minnow. As soon as you glue and clamp the body, divide the tail into two clumps, splayed out to resemble legs. Position your clamps to keep the legs separated, and let the glue cure. On this fly, I do not like the softer materials (marabou, limp synthetics, and feathers) because they often foul on the hook point.

### Sandwich Popper

**Hook:** Long-shank popper hook, size 2/0 through 8.

**Thread:** Any color.

**Tail:** Bucktail, calf tail, squirrel tail, synthetics, or saddle hackles in any color desired.

**Body:** Square or long triangle-shaped pieces of foam. To make a popper, use ¼-inch or 6 mm foam for the top, ⅛-inch or 2 mm foam for the bottom.

This is made the same way as the Sandwich Minnow, but it usually has a straight buck-tail or synthetic tail instead of the downward-curving saddles of the Sandwich Minnow. To make it pop, thicker foam is used for the top of the bug—in this case, either 6 mm or ¼-inch foam. The thicker foam makes a large enough face to let the bug pop rather than just slide or glide through the water.

Sheet foams from craft, art, and hobby stores come in two basic thicknesses, though the exact thickness might vary with the vendor or manufacturer. Some companies use metric sizes, with 2 and 6 mm being common thicknesses; others use English measurements, with ⅛- and ¼-inch thicknesses the common designations.

9

chapter

## BASIC BAITFISH

Many, but not all, saltwater flies are streamers that imitate the various baitfish found in coastal waters. They can be tied in many ways. Tying methods and styles vary according to the materials available and the size of the fly. Saltwater tying methods also vary according to the shape of the baitfish being imitated. For example, there is a big difference between the shape of a little slab-sided menhaden or shad and the round, pencil-thin shape of a sand eel. Let's look at a few of the various designs.

### The Simple One

This is fully described in the streamer chapter, but it's worth repeating here because it is such a great generic coastal pattern. It is a design that I developed some 40 years ago in an early effort to simplify my fly tying for Chesapeake Bay striper fishing.

**Hook:** Regular or long-shank stainless-steel hook, such as a Mustad 34007 or 34011, size 3/0 through 6.
**Thread:** White, black, or to match the wing color.
**Wing:** White bucktail, though other colors such as yellow, black, tan, light green, and light blue can be used. Synthetics such as Super Hair, FisHair, Neer Hair, Sexy Fiber, and others hold up better with toothy fish.

This is a one-material fly. After attaching the thread to the hook, place the wing on top of the hook shank and make two soft wraps of thread around the material. Then push down on the hair so that it surrounds or veils the hook shank. Bind the hair in place with tight wraps of thread, trim the butts of the hair, and finish wrapping the fly's head. A two-material variation has a body of tinsel, braid, chenille, or yarn wrapped down and then up the shank. A chenille, braid, or yarn body should contrast with the wing color. The one- and two-material versions tied in basic saltwater colors are very effective.

### Simple Deceiver

Lefty Kreh designed this fly in the late 1950s for striped bass in the Chesapeake Bay. It has become a standard for saltwater and warmwater fishing everywhere. The big advantage of the Deceiver style is that the feathers will not foul on the hook bend, unlike the wings of many streamer flies tied now and virtually all tied before this design. Lefty describes the fly's parts as the tail (the feathers at the rear) and the collar (the hair surrounding the front of the hook). The tail and collar work together to make a convincing baitfish silhouette while eliminating the fouling typical of feather-wing streamers.

As Lefty notes, this is not a specific pattern, but rather a design that can be tied in any size and color scheme, and even with some variations of materials. Since the collar hides the hook shank, the fly does not need a body. Lefty frequently ties Deceivers with throats of red Flashabou or Krystal Flash, toppings of Flashabou or peacock herl, some flash material on the sides, and grizzly saddle hackles along the sides of the collars. This simple version will work well in many waters.

**Hook:** Regular or long-shank stainless-steel hook, size 4/0 through 6.

**Thread:** White, black, or to match the fly's color.

**Tail:** White saddle hackles, the number based on the size of the fly. Use four hackles on small flies, six to twelve on larger flies. Tie the hackles curved in for a slim fly, or splayed out for bulk and to simulate a large baitfish.

**Collar:** White bucktail veiling the hook shank and extending back beyond the end of the hook and over the hackle-feather tail.

Attach the tail feathers first, then wrap the thread forward and tie down the collar of white bucktail. You can do this by tying down one bunch of bucktail with a few loose wraps and then pushing down on it to make the hair veil the hook, or building the collar in several parts as Lefty prefers—one clump on the far side of the hook, then one on the near side, and finally one on the top. Variations include grizzly hackles tied alongside the collar, flash tied into the collar, a red throat, or a topping that extends back over the collar and tail. You can also add painted or self-stick eyes to the heads of larger Deceivers. Naturally, you can tie these in many colors, including mixed colors.

To tie a simpliflied Lefty's Deceiver, first tie in a tail of saddle hackles. The feathers can be splayed like these, or they can be attached with their concave sides facing in.

Instead of clipping the excess hackle stems, wrap over them with the thread.

Make the collar with three small clumps of bucktail or one larger clump attached so that it veils the hook shank. Comb the bucktail before tying it to the hook. The collar should overlap the front of the tail feathers.

Finish the head. One advantage of the Deceiver style is that the tail feathers will not foul on the hook bend and spoil the fly's action in the water.

Long, thin flies like this one can imitate sand eels, spearing, or any number of slim bait-fish found in inshore waters. This is an easy, one-material fly. It can be made more complicated by adding materials, but it seldom needs extra parts to work well. Obviously, this is best tied as a sparse fly.

**Hook:** Long-shank stainless-steel or saltwater hook, size 2/0 through 4.
**Thread:** White.
**Body and tail:** White bucktail. Other colors can be used, including yellow, tan, brown, orange, pink, olive, and green. You can also use synthetics such as FisHair and Super Hair.

This entire fly consists of a wing of bucktail or similar material tied at the front and also at the bend of the hook. The second tie keeps the wing from curling around the hook bend and fouling the hook or causing the fly to spin on the cast and in the water. The secret is to attach the thread at the rear of the hook shank and leave a long tag end that you can use to make the wrap over the tail. Then wind the thread forward, tie in a sparse

To make a Simple Sand Eel, attach the thread at the rear of the hook and leave a very long tag end. Then tie in a bundle of bucktail at the head of the fly.

Trim the butts of the hair and bind them down. Note the long tag end of thread hanging from the rear of the hook.

Finish the fly's head. Whip-finish the thread and clip it.

Use the tag end of the thread to bind down the hair at the rear of the hook. This makes a slender body and a tail that will not foul on the hook.

wing of evened white bucktail, trim the butts, and finish the head. For best results, tie this wing so that it surrounds or veils the hook shank. Then turn to the rear of the fly and use the long tag end to wrap over the hair at this point. Make several wraps and tie off with a whip finish. Seal both wraps of thread.

### Tubing Sand Eel

This two-part sand eel uses the trick of starting with the sleeve of Mylar tubing slipped onto a long-tube bobbin. By starting this way, you can complete the fly in two quick, easy tying steps.

**Hook:** Long-shank stainless-steel or saltwater hook, size 1/0 through 4.
**Thread:** White.
**Wing:** White bucktail. You can also use tan, yellow, pink, orange, light green, or brown bucktail, or you can tie the fly with synthetic hair in any of these colors.
**Body:** A sleeve of Mylar tubing, equal to the shank length of the hook.

To make a Tubing Sand Eel, begin by slipping a piece of Mylar tubing onto the bobbin tube. When you attach the thread to the hook, leave a long tag end for wrapping the rear of the body tubing.

Attach a bundle of combed and stacked bucktail. The Mylar tubing is still on the bobbin.

Slide the Mylar tubing up the thread and onto the hook. Tie down the front of the tubing.

Use the long tag end of thread to wrap the rear of the tubing to secure it. Whip-finish the thread, and coat both wraps with head cement.

Start by measuring a piece of Mylar tubing equal to the shank length of the hook. This should be very slim tubing, not the larger tubing used for some other flies. Slide the Mylar tubing onto the bobbin tube. Then tie down the thread (with the Mylar tubing on the bobbin), clip the excess, and tie in a sparse wing of bucktail. Clip the excess bucktail. Then spool the bobbin to position the end of the tube next to the hook eye and slide the Mylar tubing up onto the hook shank and over the just-tied wing. Tie down the front of the Mylar tubing, make a neat head, and whip-finish. Add stick-on eyes if desired and seal the head with head cement or epoxy. The tail end of the Mylar tubing will fray a little, but this will only add more flash to the fly. The tubing also prevents the bucktail wing from fouling on the hook. If you want to prevent the tubing from fraying, you can use the technique for the Simple Sand Eel (above); begin by attaching the thread at the rear of the hook shank, and leave a long tag end with which you can tie down the bucktail and the rear end of the tubing after finishing the rest of the fly.

### Quick Minnow

This fly makes use of the same tubing-on-the-bobbin trick, but it calls for larger, woven tubing rather than Mylar. Unlike the Tubing Sand Eel, the Quick Minnow is a generic baitfish pattern. The wing can consist of natural material such as bucktail, a synthetic such as Super Hair, feathers, or a combination of these. One favorite technique is to tie a wing and a topping, and then slide the tubing in place to complete the fly. The result is still a three-material fly, but it has the color scheme typical of baitfish—light below and darker above. You can make the topping with peacock herl, darker bucktail, or dark synthetic hair. Quick Minnows can be tied in bright or light colors and in dark, somber colors to simulate anything from glass minnows to bottom-feeding sculpins.

**Hook:** Regular or long-shank (depending upon the minnow being imitated) stainless-steel or saltwater hook, size 3/0 through 4.
**Thread:** White, or to match the other materials.
**Wing:** Bucktail, synthetic hair, saddle hackles, or a combination of these, about twice the length of the hook shank, in colors ranging from white through black.
**Topping** (optional): A darker material to add shading to the fly. Use peacock herl or dark bucktail or synthetic hair.
**Body:** A sleeve of E-Z Body or Corsair; pick a diameter that works with the size of the fly.

Cut a piece of tubing the length of the hook shank. To keep the end of the tubing from fraying, use a fly-tying cauterizing tool, cutting the material at an angle at the tail end. Then slide the tubing onto the bobbin, and attach the thread to the front of the hook shank. Tie in the wing material and topping. Turn the thread spool backwards to bring the mouth of the bobbin to the hook eye so that you can slide the tubing onto the hook shank. With the tubing in place, wrap over the front end of the material to bind it down, make the head, and tie off. A variation is to add self-stick eyes and coat the head with clear epoxy.

The tubing used for this fly comes in different sizes and shades. When placed over the wing material, the tubing makes for a scaly finish that looks very minnow-like. If you wish to make a flat minnow, iron a three-foot length of tubing on a hard kitchen counter.

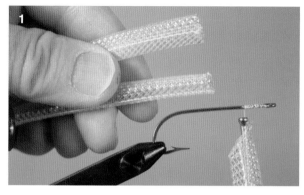

A Quick Minnow uses plastic tubing such as E-Z Body or Corsair for the body. Cut a piece of tubing to length and slip it onto the bobbin. Attach the thread to the hook.

Note that the rear edge of the tubing is cut at an angle.

Tie in the wing/tail material. You can use a synthetic material such as Super Hair or a natural material such as bucktail.

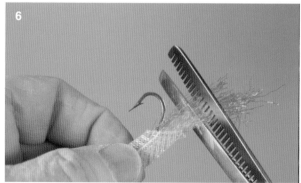

With the bobbin close to the hook eye, slide the tubing up onto the hook to cover the front of the wing/tail. The wing color shows through the tubing to give the fly a translucent look.

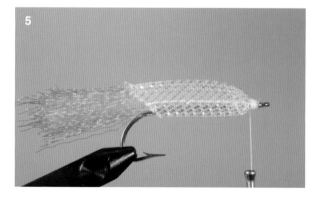

Tie down the front end of the tubing and make the head of the fly. Whip-finish, clip, and seal the thread. Add eyes if you want them.

To give the wing a tapered, more natural look, use barber's thinning shears to cut some of the fibers.

The tapered wing (bottom) looks more natural than a bundle of hair trimmed straight across.

Position the threads running lengthwise through the tubing on each side and color them with a Sharpie marker to make lateral lines. Pressing a long length of tubing like this makes it quick and easy to cut off what you need when tying flies.

Easy Seaducer

A Seaducer is little more than a hackle-feather tail with a hackle collar. The early saltwater fly fisher Homer Rhode used them for tarpon and other fish (he called them Shrimp Flies), but the earliest Seaducer-style flies were used for largemouth fishing in the South. Nowadays, Seaducers are used mostly for saltwater fishing, but they remain equally good for largemouths, smallmouths, pike, crappies, shad (in small sizes), and other gamefish. They can be tied in any color and size.

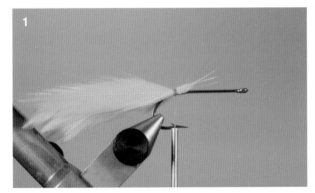

To make an Easy Seaducer, first tie in a tail of splayed saddle hackles.

It's important to tie the tail feathers as far back on the hook shank as possible to keep them from fouling. After attaching the feathers, clip the excess stems and bind them down.

Tie in one or more saddle hackles to make the body. Wrap the hackles up the hook shank and tie them off at the front of the hook. Complete the head and whip-finish.

**Hook:** Regular-length stainless-steel or saltwater hook, size 3/0 through 8.
**Thread:** Black, red, to match the color of the fly, or to contrast with the fly's color.
**Tail/wing:** A bundle of saddle hackles, tied just forward of the bend of the hook. Any color or combination of colors of saddle hackles can be used.
**Collar:** Matching or contrasting hackle tightly palmered and filling the hook shank.

You can use any color for tails and collars. Popular colors include white, yellow, red, black, medium green, medium blue, brown, pink, and orange. Popular patterns are all white, all yellow, all black, red and white, black and white, green and yellow, green and white, brown and tan, and brown and white. Variations include adding lead to the hook shank to get the fly deep, adding Flashabou or other flash to the tail for added sparkle, and adding a topping of peacock herl to the tail/wing before wrapping the collar.

### Easy Whistler

This fly by Dan Blanton, a West Coast tier, angler, and writer, at first seems like a bucktail version of a Seaducer, but it is actually very different from the Seaducer. One difference is in the bulk of the materials; a standard Whistler has a heavy clump of bucktail and a plump wrap of chenille behind the collar. Another difference is the Whistler's large bead-chain or dumbbell eyes that help get the fly deep.

On our simple version, we will leave out the Flashabou and the red chenille gills found on standard Whistlers. You can, of course, add any flash material to the tail and weight the fly with metal eyes or lead wire wrapped on the hook shank. Even with the additon of these materials, a Whistler remains a relatively simple fly, though it does exceed the three-material limit of this book.

The main advantage of this fly is its bulk, which produces vibrations or pulses that attract fish, particularly in stained water or under low-light conditions. Thanks to the bead-chain or dumbbell eyes at the front of a standard-length or short-shank hook, the fly will dip during a pause in the retrieve. A Whistler fished with a twitching, stop-and-go retrieve has a lot of action.

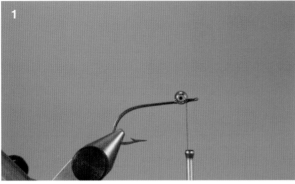

Begin an Easy Whistler by attaching the thread at the front of the hook and then tying in dumbbell or bead-chain eyes.

Wind the thread to the rear and tie in a bundle of combed bucktail. On a large fly, you might want to build the tail with three clumps of hair. Wrap up and back to cover the butt ends of the hair.

Attach at least one hackle feather for wrapping over the hook shank.

Wrap the hackle up to the eyes. Tie off the feather behind the bead chain or dumbbell. Clip the excess, make a few more wraps, and whip-finish the thread.

**Hook:** Regular or short-shank stainless-steel or saltwater hook, size 4/0 through 2.

**Thread:** Red, black, or to match the collar.

**Eyes:** Large stainless-steel bead-chain or a metal dumbbell. Besides lead, dumbbells are manufactured of brass and tin.

**Tail/wing:** Bucktail, tied densely at the rear of the hook shank. Popular colors include white, yellow, black, light green, brown, and tan.

**Collar:** Large hackle feathers tightly palmered up the hook shank to the bead chain or dumbbell. The color can match or contrast with the tail/wing; popular colors include white, yellow, black, red, dark green, and brown.

Attach the bead-chain or dumbbell eyes first, and then spiral-wrap the thread to the rear of the hook shank and add the dense tail/wing. To make the tail, tie in several bundles of hair. Comb the fuzz and short hairs out of a clump of bucktail and bind the hair to the far side of the hook. Add another clump of cleaned hair on the near side of the hook, and then tie a third bundle on top of the shank. To add bulk to the fly, let the butt ends of the hair extend to just in back of the eyes. Tie in the several saddle hackles necessary to make the collar, and then wrap the thread over the butt ends of the bucktail all the way up to the bead chain or dumbbell. Wrap the hackle tightly up the hook shank to make a bushy, bulky collar that will move a lot of water when the fly is retrieved.

### Bluefish Special

I developed this fly about 40 years ago to cope with the sharp teeth of bluefish in the Chesapeake Bay. These fish, ranging from a few to 15 or more pounds, offer some great fly fishing, but with teeth that rival those of a piranha, they chew up a fly in short order, usually cutting the thread holding the fly together. My simple solution is a one-material fly consisting of a clump of hair tied to the rear of a long-shank hook. The long, bare hook shank serves as a built-in bite tippet. Although I tied Bluefish Specials with bucktail for many years, I have switched to Super Hair and other synthetics unavailable 40 years ago. This change, along with an epoxy head coating, makes for a longer-lasting fly.

A Bluefish Special is tied at the very rear of a long-shank hook. Attach a bundle of natural or synthetic hair; this is white bucktail.

Add another clump of hair to give the fly a dark back. This one has three colors: white, yellow, and black. Tie off the thread and coat the wrap with epoxy.

To make fancier and more durable flies, use synthetic hair, flash material, and stick-on prismatic or 3-D eyes.

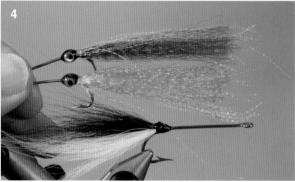

Whether it's simple of fancy, natural or plastic, a Bluefish Special has a long, bare shank that serves as a built-in bite tippet. These are good flies for all toothy fish.

**Hook:** Long-shank stainless-steel or saltwater hook such as a Mustad 34011, size 3/0 through 2.

**Thread:** Black or red.

**Wing/tail:** Bucktail or synthetic hair in any of the basic saltwater colors. Synthetics such as Super Hair last longer than natural hair. You can add a topping or back of black, dark blue, dark green, or violet Super Hair.

Attach the thread and tie in the wing at the very rear of the hook shank. Add the topping if you want the fly to have a dark back, and then wrap a short, tapered head. Finish with a coat of epoxy on the head of the fly. An option is to add self-stick, doll, or prismatic eyes glued to the head before the clear epoxy coating. The advantages of this fly are the tough synthetic wing, the impervious epoxy-coated head, and the length of heavy-wire hook shank that serves as a short bite tippet. If you're fishing for big fish or aggressive, gulping blues, you may have to add a 3-inch wire leader to the eye of the fly to protect the mono tippet.

### Still Blonde

The legendary Joe Brooks is credited with designing the Blondes, a type of saltwater fly that consists of a long tail, tinsel body, and long wing. Brooks tied the first Blondes long before the arrival of the many synthetics available now, and he didn't have such materials as Flashabou, Mylar tinsels, Krystal Flash, holographic flash materials, tinsel braids for bodies, and so on. You can add any of these to the wing or tail of a Blonde if you like. You can also change the tinsel body to one of the many round or flat braided materials available today in many colors.

**Hook:** Regular or long-shank stainless-steel or saltwater hook such as a Mustad 34007 or 34011, size 4/0 through 6.

**Thread:** Black.

**Tail:** A long, full clump of bucktail.

**Body:** Silver tinsel.

**Wing:** A long, full wing matching the density and length of the tail, and in the same or a contrasting color. The ends of the wing and tail should meet.

Joe came up with a number of different patterns, including the Argentine Blonde (blue/white), Blushing Blonde (red-orange/white), Honey Blonde (all yellow), Hot Orange Blonde (orange), Integration Blonde (black/white), Irish Blonde (light green/white), and Platinum Blonde (all white). The yellow and orange patterns usually used gold tinsel instead of silver. This design can be tied upside down so that the wing protects and hides the hook point. Modern variations are to tie Blondes with synthetics such as Super Hair, FisHair, or Aqua Fiber, and to use flat or round braid for the body.

The secret to tying Blondes, particularly with tinsel bodies, is to tie in the tail so that the butts extend to the tie-down point for the wing. Attach the thread to the hook, tie in the tail, and then tie in the tinsel. Wrap the thread forward over the butt ends of the tail hair to provide an even base for the tinsel, and wrap the tinsel over the smooth base. Tie off the tinsel and clip the excess, attach the wing hair, and wrap the fly's head. Failure to extend the tail butts will result in a lumpy, uneven body. The fish won't care, but your friends will laugh at you.

To tie a simple, three-material Blonde as originated by Joe Brooks, first attach a tail of combed, evened bucktail. Leave the butt ends long and cover them with a wrap of thread. Tie in the tinsel for the body.

Wrap the tinsel forward to evenly cover the hook shank.

Add a wing of combed, evened bucktail. The wing should be as long as the tail.

Finish the head. Whip-finish the thread and coat the head with cement. Note the lengths of the tail and wing; they're the same.

One mistake in tying Blondes is cutting off the tail butts like these. Trimming the butts too short makes a big lump on the hook.

The lump leads to a very uneven wrap of tinsel. The fish might not care, but your friends will laugh at you.

Like the Lefty's Deceiver, this is another fly that will almost never foul on the cast. With only two materials, it is very easy to tie. Mark Sosin, an angling author and TV personality, relates that he developed the fly when he was living in New Jersey in the 1960s. He invented the Blossom style not for a specific fish, but as a slow-retrieve or twitch-retrieve fly that would have action even when at rest, thanks to its marabou tail. It is essentially a saltwater version of a Woolly Bugger, minus the palmered hackle.

**Hook:** Long-shank stainless-steel or saltwater hook, size 4/0 through 6.
**Thread:** Black or to match the color of the fly.
**Tail:** A full clump of marabou in basic colors including white, yellow, black, and pink.
**Body:** Chenille. The diameter of the chenille depends on the size of the hook, but a Blossom always has a thick body. The body color can match or contrast with the marabou tail.

Mark Sosin's Blossom is like a simple Woolly Bugger designed for salt water. Start by tying in a clump of marabou for the tail. Attach a length of chenille.

Wrap the thread forward and follow it with the wrap of chenille.

Although it's very simple, the completed Blossom will catch many saltwater species.

You can't beat this fly for action, though toothy fish will chew up the marabou in a hurry. The original Blossoms had matching bodies and tails, but you can also make them contrast. Contrasting body/tail colors that I like are red/white, green/yellow, brown/tan, red/pink, orange/yellow, and black/white. Variations include adding a little flash material (Flashabou, Krystal Flash, and the like) to the tail, using Estaz or Cactus Chenille for the body, and palmering the body to make a saltwater Woolly Bugger.

### Bend-Back Flies

Bend-back flies are old styles tied upside down on hooks that are bent in back of the eye. As a result of this bent hook, the wing hides and protects the hook point; thanks to the upside-down orientation, the fly avoids many snags. Bend-backs are more fully described in chapter 5, "Simple Streamers."

**Hook:** Long-shank stainless-steel hook such as a Mustad 34011, bent ¼ inch in back of the hook eye. The size can range from 2/0 through 6.
**Thread:** White or to match the wing color.
**Wing:** Bucktail; white, yellow, black, shad, light green, and light blue are all good colors. Synthetics in the same colors are also ideal for this fly.

You can buy special Bend-back hooks or make your own. To modify a long-shank hook, hold it behind the eye with needle-nose pliers and bend the shank slightly.

Bend-backs lend themsevles to many variations. You can add a dark back (black, dark blue, dark green, or violet), flash material such as Flashabou or Krystal Flash, or a red throat of calf tail. You can also add prism, doll, or self-stick eyes to the head of the fly, gluing them on and then covering the head with clear epoxy.

### Mostly Menhaden

Menhaden, called bunker and pogies in some areas, are great baitfish and a staple food of many gamefish. They will grow to a foot or more in length, but all sizes of menhaden are used as bait, and many lures have been designed to imitate them. Fly tiers have devised many fly patterns that imitate these slab-sided fish. This one is a very easy tie. Depending upon how big you make it and what color materials you use, this simple fly can imitate menhaden, small shad, cunner, butterfish, crevalles, alewife, blueback herring, mullet, mummichogs, sheepshead minnows, snapper bluefish, or killifish. You can vary the look by using different colors and by adding markings with a permanent marker.

**Hook:** Long-shank saltwater or stainless-steel hook, size 3/0 through 6.
**Thread:** Cream, yellow, or to match the Body Fur.
**Tail:** Long-fibered Body Fur or synthetic hair.
**Body:** Standard Body Fur.
**Eyes:** Doll, prism, or self-stick eyes.

Body Fur, a great material from Dan Bailey and others, comes in both long and short versions. The short form is like rug fringe without the rug, and wraps around a hook shank like a synthetic hackle. It also comes in long form for making wings and tails. To tie a Mostly Menhaden, attach the thread at the rear of the hook shank and tie down a short piece of the long-fibered Body Fur. You can substitute other materials, particularly if you want a different tail color or some flash in the tail. Then tie in a length of short-fibered Body Fur, wind the thread forward, and wrap the Body Fur. Complete the head and tie off, then glue on eyes to complete the fly.

You can leave a Mostly Menhaden plain or mark it with a felt-tip marker to give it vertical bars (killifish, mummichogs, sheepshead minnows) or a darker back (white perch, menhaden, bluefish, blueback herring). Tie it in colors ranging from white or shad for white perch through dark brown for cunner and sculpin patterns.

Begin a Mostly Menhaden by attaching the tail to the hook. You can make the tail with a piece of long-fibered Body Fur or with a clump of synthetic hair.

Tie on a length of Body Fur, a material that resembles a synthetic hackle and can be wrapped around a hook shank. Wind the thread forward.

Wrap the Body Fur around the hook shank, spiraling it forward all the way to the front of the hook. Make sure that the fibers lie to the rear.

Tie off the Body Fur and clip the excess. Glue the eyes to the head. In the water, this simple fly represents a deep-bodied baitfish.

### SIMPLE FLIES FOR CHUMMING

Chumming is a controversial subject among fly fishers. Some endorse anything that will (legally) bring fish within range, and others completely oppose using chum. Chumming is using an attractant to bring fish to the boat or fishing location so that they are concentrated and more easily taken with a fly. Whether it is ground fish, live baitfish, dead shrimp, pieces of clams or crabs, or merely a scent released into the water, chum also makes gamefish more receptive to artificial flies. Chumming is widely used for striped bass and bluefish in the Chesapeake Bay, and it is a popular method in many other areas. Any pattern can be used as a "chum fly," but you can also tie flies specifically to resemble the bits of fish flesh ground up and used as chum in many places.

#### Chum Fly

This chum fly can be tied quickly and easily with one material, or it can be toughened up with epoxy if it is to be used for bluefish. Adding epoxy to this simple fly doesn't make much sense unless you are fishing only for blues and want to eke out another fish or two per fly.

**Hook:** Standard-length stainless-steel hook, size 2/0 through 4.
**Thread:** Black or to match the rabbit fur.
**Body:** A cross-cut rabbit strip in a color to match the ground fish bait. Tan, brown, gray, red, pink, and orange are all good.

This is an easy fly to tie, though it does produce tufts of errant rabbit fur flying around your workbench. Secure the thread to the rear of the hook shank, and tie in the end of cross-cut rabbit strip. Taper the skin at the end of the strip for easy tying, and make sure that you tie in the right end so that the fur will point toward the rear of the hook as you wrap the strip around the shank. Once you have secured the strip, wrap the thread to the forward part of the hook, and then wrap the rabbit strip in a tight spiral. Tie off the strip, clip the excess, and whip-finish the thread. Seal the thread wraps with head cement.

To make this kind of fly last longer when you fish for bluefish or other toothy critters, first mix a puddle of slow-setting epoxy. Attach the rabbit strip to the hook, and coat the tie-on point and the hook shank with epoxy before wrapping the rabbit skin forward. Then wrap forward, laying the rabbit skin in the epoxy to glue it to the hook shank. Seal the "head" with epoxy before putting the fly on a rotator. The result is a bulletproof fly, but one that takes a little longer than the original to tie. The reason for using slow-setting epoxy rather than the five-minute kind is to have time to tie a half-dozen or more flies before the epoxy sets. Five-minute epoxy will give you time to tie only one fly before you have to mix another batch.

To begin a Chum Fly, attach the thread at the rear of the hook and then tie in a cross-cut rabbit strip. Wrap the thread forward.

Spiral-wrap the cross-cut rabbit strip around the hook shank, almost like you were palmering a hackle. Stroke the fur rearward as you wrap. Tie off the strip at the front of the hook.

Clip the excess rabbit and tie off the thread. The fly is meant to resemble a piece of chum; it is cast into a chum line after fish show up to enjoy the free lunch.

# chapter
# 10

**BASIC SHRIMP PATTERNS**

Shrimp are a staple of many saltwater species. They are meals for many inshore and offshore species, including stripers, bluefish, redfish, seatrout, cobia, bonefish, permit, tarpon, and snook. Shrimp live in all the world's oceans, and they range in size from tiny inshore species to large species whose bodies resemble those of small lobsters. Most imitations for fly fishing will range from about 1 to 3 inches long.

Flies that resemble shrimp are particularly important to anglers who fish in warm and tropical waters. Many shrimp patterns are complex, often having a half-dozen to a dozen materials and long tying instructions. But a couple of simple patterns work just as well as more complicated lures do, and they require only a few minutes to tie.

Simple Shrimp

This shrimp pattern is tied with three materials, or four if you want to include eyes. But the instructions are simple and the tying is quick and easy. This fly employs some synthetic materials that are readily available, though not always in fly shops. One of them is a transparent vinyl that comes in clear, rose, yellow, blue, and green. Most sewing, fabric, and craft stores carry it. You can buy as little as ⅛ of a yard of this vinyl, giving you a piece measuring 4¼ inches times the width of the roll (36 to 54 inches, depending upon the supplier), which is a lot of fly-tying material. I cut the big piece into smaller patches, each about the size of a dollar bill, for easy handling. You can also use products such as cloth-backed vinyl, Furry Foam, Thin Skin, Bug Skin, and similar materials that are easy to trim into the shape of the shrimp's carapace.

Use plastic, rounded-end bristles from a hair brush for the eyes. You can find this type of hair brush at the nearest discount or "dollar" store. Just make sure that the bristles are plastic and not metal. You turn the bristles into eyes by cutting off two and binding one stalk on each side of the fly's head.

**Hook:** Long shank, stainless steel, size 1/0 through 6.
**Thread:** To match the fly's color, or a contrasting color if you want the carapace segmentation to stand out.
**Eyes:** Plastic hair-brush bristles extending in back of the hook bend, or V-shaped mono eyes as described in chapter 2.
**Body:** First, a clump of Super Hair or Unique bound along the hook shank. Use a clump long enough so that one end will stick out in front of the hook eye about ¼ of an inch, and the other end will extend beyond the hook bend about three-fourths of the shank length. Use Super Hair (0.004 thickness) for larger flies, and Unique (0.003 thickness) for smaller flies. The best colors are yellow, white, pink, chartreuse, salmon, orange, light green, and tan. After tying the synthetic hair to the hook, wrap the shank with Cactus Chenille or Estaz the same color as the Super Hair or Unique.
**Carapace:** A piece of clear, rose, yellow, green, or blue vinyl cut to the shape shown in the photos. Although shrimp can move either forward or backward, this pattern is tied with the tail at the front of the

hook to resemble a fleeing shrimp. Once you've decided on the colors and materials, prepare eyes and trim carapaces for a bunch of shrimp. With the parts prepared, you can then assemble flies rapidly.

After attaching the thread to the hook, tie a hair-brush bristle on each side of the hook bend. Tie these pointing to the rear of the fly, then bend each stem outward slightly so that the round eyes will be visible on the sides of the head. Cut a bundle of Super Hair or Unique about twice the length of the hook. Position it so that about ¼ of an inch extends in front of the hook eye, with the rest along the shank and in back of the hook. Spiral-wrap the synthetic hair to secure it to the hook, ending up at the bend of the hook. Tie in a length of Cactus Chenille, spiral-wrap the thread to the hook eye, and wrap the chenille. Tie off and clip the excess chenille. Push the Super Hair at the front of the hook down and under the shank so that it will look like a tail. Trim the vinyl carapace to shape (with practice, you can prepare a bunch of these in advance) and poke a hole in the tail

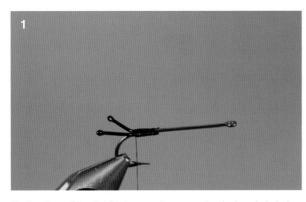

To begin a Simple Shrimp, cut some plastic brush bristles (the kind with knobby ends) and tie two in place—one on each side of the rear of the hook shank.

Tie down a clump of material that will make the head of the shrimp (between the eyes) and also the tail (under the hook eye). Synthetic hair works well.

Cut out a carapace from clear or translucent vinyl to cover the shrimp. A template (left) can simplify this step and help produce consistent parts. Punch a hole in the tail end to fit over the hook eye.

Wrap the hook with Cactus Chenille, and then force the hole in the vinyl carapace over the hook eye. Lay the carapace on top of the body and wrap it with thread to make segments. Tie off with a whip finish.

All that remains on this fly is to whip-finish the thread. Although it doesn't have many parts, a Simple Shrimp is a convincing imitation.

end. Push the vinyl over the hook eye, and then make several wraps of thread to hold the vinyl tail in place over the Super Hair. Holding the carapace on top of the body, spiral-wrap the thread around the body, taking two turns at each segment to define the carapace and hold it in place. Finish at the head of the fly (the rear of the hook), and tie off with a whip finish. Coat the thread wraps on top of the carapace with head cement.

### Silly Shrimp

This shrimp is made like the preceding one, except that the carapace is clear silicone sealer/glue molded onto the body. Make the mold from a flexible corrugated or ridged plastic (ideally, polyethylene) drinking straw. Cut the straw into pieces, and then slice each piece lengthwise to make a ridged mold. The mold will give the silicone sealer its shape.

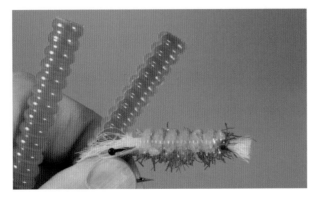

The back of a Silly Shrimp is a layer of silicone sealer molded to shape by a piece cut from a corrugated, bendable drinking straw. Tie most of the fly like the Simple Shrimp, but do not add the vinyl carapace. Cut a corrugated plastic straw into sections, and then cut the sections lengthwise to make molds (two are shown in the photo). Apply a bead of silicone sealer to the back of the fly. Press the fly into the mold. After the sealer has cured, remove the mold.

**Hook:** Long shank, stainless steel, size 1/0 through 6.

**Thread:** To match the fly's color, or a contrasting color to make the carapace segmentation more visible.

**Eyes:** A pair of plastic hair-brush bristles extending beyond the hook bend.

**Body:** As on the Simple Shrimp, a clump of Super Hair or Unique bound along the hook shank. Use a clump long enough so that one end will stick out in front of the hook eye about ¼ of an inch and the other end will extend beyond the hook bend about three fourths of the shank length. Use Super Hair (0.004 thickness) for larger flies, and Unique (0.003 thickness) for smaller flies. The best colors are yellow, white, pink, chartreuse, salmon, orange, light green, and tan. After tying the synthetic hair to the hook, wrap the shank with Cactus Chenille or Estaz the same color as the Super Hair or Unique.

**Carapace:** Clear silicone sealer applied to the top of the body and molded to shape with the "flex" part of a plastic drinking straw.

The main part of this fly is tied exactly like the Simple Shrimp. In fact, this fly was the precursor of that fly. The difference between the two is that instead of being tied, the Silly Shrimp's carapace is molded. Once the body of the fly is complete, place a thin bead of clear silicone sealer on top of the chenille body. Then place the fly with the hook point up into the mold made from the flexible part of a plastic drinking straw that was cut in half lengthwise. The mold shapes the silicone sealer into ridges that approximate the ridges or segments of a real shrimp. Once the sealer has cured, remove the fly from the mold.

Both of these shrimp flies are fished the same way, either by blind-casting into areas frequented by gamefish and shrimp, or by sight-casting to specific fish or schools of fish and working the fly with a slow, rhythmic retrieve that simulates the backward motion of a fleeing shrimp.

### BASIC CRAB PATTERNS

Many of us enjoy the blue crabs popular along the East Coast. They're served steamed, in crab cakes, as soft shells, and in crab imperial. Gamefish enjoy small crabs of the same species, juvenile crabs of other species, and all smaller varieties of crabs. Crabs are *not* just for permit—all species of inshore fish will eat them. Best are the small crabs that measure an inch or two across the points. Larger crabs are eaten by fish and used as bait by fishermen (as when bottom fishing for black drum), but an imitation of a 4- or 5-inch crab is hardly a practical fly. Blue crabs, mud crabs, green crabs, mole crabs, sand crabs, fiddler crabs, and all the related species are relished by inshore gamefish. As they have with shrimp flies, fly tiers have devised many complex and time-consuming patterns for crabs, but the following flies satisfy the needs of most anglers and are easy and quick to tie.

#### Sandwich Sinking Crab

Small crabs often float in or just below the surface, swimming sideways with the current. When they perceive danger, they dive for the bottom, where they stay until the threat passes, or until a fish finds them. This crab pattern has the weight on one end, which causes it to sink at angle. It's ideal for bonefish and permit, which often seek crabs and other prey on the bottom.

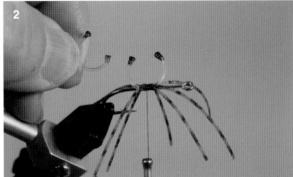

Begin a Simple Crab by attaching some rubber legs to the center of the hook shank.

Add horseshoe-shaped monofilament eyes. Instructions for making these eyes are in chapter 2.

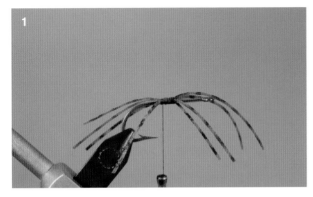

The eyes stick out from the side of the hook shank. Whip-finish and clip the thread; you're done tying.

Cut the carapace and belly from pieces of cloth-backed vinyl. The carapace is darker than the belly piece.

Glue one piece of cloth-backed vinyl to the hook, and then add the second piece, sandwiching the hook, legs, and eye stalks between the belly and carapace.

Before the glue sets, check the legs and spread them out if necessary. Use doll clothespins to clamp the parts until the glue cures.

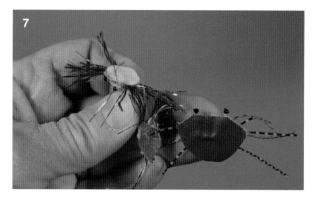

The same sandwich technique lets you make fast-sinking crabs with dumbbell weights, suspending crabs, and floating crabs. These flies appeal to most inshore gamefish.

**Hook:** Regular length, stainless steel, size 1 through 6.

**Thread:** Any color.

**Weight:** A metal dumbbell tied to the hook or a cone head slid onto the hook (bend down the barb) before tying. A dumbbell tied to the top of the hook shank helps the fly turn over and ride point up. Use a small dumbbell for still conditions and shallow water, and a heavier dumbbell for deeper water and fast currents.

**Eyes:** Mono eyes (see chapter 2 for instructions on making horseshoe-shaped eyes). These are really an option; you can tie the fly without them.

**Legs:** Silicone, Lumaflex, or rubber material such as that used for legs on bass bugs or skirts on spinnerbaits. Mottled or banded legs look best, in colors such as orange, brown, tan, black, or green.

**Body:** Cloth-backed vinyl (such as chair upholstery or Naugahyde) in tan, light green, brown, gray, cream, and other colors for the back or carapace, and in cream for the belly. Similar materials such as Bug Skin or Pleather may be used.

This fly is glued as much as tied, but it's still very simple to make. Attach the thread at the front of the hook, and tie the dumbbell weight on top of the shank in back of the hook eye. Move the thread back to the center of the hook and tie in the horseshoe eyes (see chapter 2) so that the eyes are aimed to the side, at right angles to the plane of the hook. Then tie in a bundle of silicone or rubber legs. Whip-finish and clip the thread. If you want to, you can tie a number of crab flies up to this stage.

Completing the fly involves gluing the vinyl body. Cut out the carapace and belly from cloth-backed vinyl after making their outlines with an ellipse template. Apply glue (Ultra Flex is good) to the pieces, and sandwich the hook between them with the body at right angles to the hook's plane. Clamp the parts with doll clothespins (available in a toy or doll store), and fan out the legs on both sides of the body so that they resemble the appendages of a swimming crab. Allow the glue to cure.

### Sandwich Suspended Crab

**Hook:** Regular length, stainless steel, size 1 through 6.

**Thread:** Any color.

**Eyes:** Mono eyes (see chapter 2 for instructions on making horseshoe-shaped eyes). These are really an option; you can tie the fly without them.

**Legs:** Silicone, Lumaflex, or rubber material such as that used for legs on bass bugs or skirts on spinnerbaits. Mottled or banded legs look best, in colors such as orange, brown, tan, black, or green.

**Body:** Cloth-backed vinyl (such as chair upholstery or Naugahyde) in tan, light green, brown, gray, cream, and other colors for the back or carapace, and in cream for the belly. Similar materials such as Bug Skin or Pleather may be used.

Tie this just like the fast-sinking version, but without the dumbbell weight. Other materials can be used for the body, including Fuzzy Foam or similar fly-tying "skin" materials. Lacking any extra weight, this fly will sink slowly; on a twitching retrieve, it will suspend or swim just under the surface, as do many baby crabs.

### Simple Floater Crab

**Hook:** Regular length, stainless steel, size 1 through 6.

**Thread:** Any color.

**Legs:** Lumaflex or rubber leg material.

**Body:** Thin craft or fly-tying foam (about 2 mm or ¹⁄₁₆ to ⅛ inch) in tan, yellow, brown, gray, or cream for the crab's carapace, and in cream for the belly.

This is another sandwich crab, but it's made with pieces of sheet foam instead of vinyl or Fuzzy Foam. The foam will keep the fly in the surface film. To make a crab that barely floats, use foam for the back (carapace) and cloth-backed vinyl or Fuzzy Foam for the belly.

## SIMPLE BONEFISH FLIES

Bonefish flies can, and do, fill entire books. They range from detailed shrimp and crabs through the many variations of the Crazy Charlie tied with their points up and with wings of natural or synthetic hair. Lifelike crab and shrimp patterns work well for bonefish, but so do many simpler patterns. Tan, pink, yellow, white, and orange are effective colors. By varying the colors and weights of the following styles, a bonefish angler can stock several boxes with good flies that will work in many places.

### Simply Charlie

**Hook:** Regular length, stainless steel, size 2 through 8.

**Thread:** Tan, pink, or yellow, according to the wing color.

**Eyes:** Stainless-steel bead chain. Variations include lead or lead-free dumbbell eyes, cone heads, and plastic beads.

**Body:** Braid material such as that from Gudebrod or Kreinik in pink, yellow, tan, white, cream, light green, or orange. Variations include yarn, EZ-Dub, chenille, Ultra Chenille, and Larva Lace or another plastic body wrap in the same colors.

**Wing:** White, yellow, cream, light green, pink, or tan calf tail. Variations include flash materials such as Krystal Flash or Crystal Splash, synthetic fibers such as Unique or FisHair, short bucktail, and hackle feathers.

The original Crazy Charlie has a more complicated body made of monofilament or clear vinyl wrapped over tinsel, but the basic design serves as the basis of a number of bonefish flies. This simple version has only three materials, counting the bead-chain eyes. The construction is obvious. Attach the thread to the hook, tie the eyes on top of the shank, and then tie in the body material. Wind the body material back and then forward, and tie off and clip the excess braid. Tie in the wing, trim the wing butts, and finish the head.

To tie a Simply Charlie bonefish fly, start with the hook point up. Attach dumbbell or bead-chain eyes, and then tie in a length of body material.

Wrap the body material down and then back up the hook shank.

Attach the wing material on the same side as the hook point. Trim the wing butts and finish the head.

These bonefish flies vary in color, weight, and materials, but they are all tied the same way.

## Charlie with a Tail

**Hook:** Regular length, stainless steel, size 2 through 8.

**Thread:** Pink, yellow, tan, white, chartreuse, light green, or orange.

**Eyes:** Stainless-steel bead chain. Variations include lead or lead-free dumbbell eyes, cone heads, and plastic beads.

**Tail:** A few short strands of flash material in silver, pink, yellow, pearlescent, chartreuse, and other colors. The same material is used for the wing. Variations include using synthetics such as white, yellow, cream, light green, pink, or tan Unique or FisHair instead of flash material.

**Body:** Braid, yarn, EZ-Dub, chenille, Ultra Chenille, Larva Lace, and so forth in the same colors as for the Simply Charlie.

**Wing:** The same material used for the tail.

On this fly, the tail and wing are made from the same bundle of material. After securing the bead chain, turn the hook over and tie a clump of flash material (or synthetic hair) along the hook shank. One end of the clump becomes the fly's tail; the other end sticks out in front of the hook eye and will become the wing. Attach and wrap the body material. After making the body, fold the forward-pointing flash material or synthetic hair to the rear so that it becomes a wing, and bind the material in place. Even though the fly has one additional part, it has the same number of materials as the Simply Charlie.

One clump of flash material can become a bonefish fly's tail and wing. After tying eyes to the hook, bind a long clump of flash material along the inside of the shank. Wrap the body. Note that the forward end of the flash material is sticking out of the front of the fly.

To finish the Charlie with a Tail, fold the flash material back and bind it in place to make the wing. Tie off the thread. If necessary, trim the wing and tail to length.

### Skipping Shrimp

**Hook:** Long shank, stainless steel, sizes 2 through 8.

**Thread:** Tan, white, cream, yellow, or chartreuse.

**Eyes:** Dumbbell, bead chain, plastic beads, or cone head.

**Tail:** Braided body material in a light color such as silver, pearlescent, yellow, gold, tan, cream, or white.

**Collar:** Grizzly hackle.

**Body:** The same material used for the tail.

This fly looks like a shrimp scurrying along the bottom. Tying it begins with securing the eyes on top of the hook shank. Then tie in the tail by attaching a long piece of braided body material such as one of those from Gudebrod, Kreinik, and other companies. You can begin with a long tail, since you can trim it later. Wrap the material to the hook and secure with several tight wraps of thread. Tie in a grizzly hackle, wrap it, and tie off the feather. Tie off and clip the excess hackle and finish the fly's head. Use a bodkin to fray the braided material that forms the fly's tail. The eyes and the absence of a wing make this fly look totally different from a Crazy Charlie style, but it still has a profile that bonefish like. The hackle collar has a lot of action as you retrieve the fly across the bottom.

Another way to make a tailed bonefish fly is to tie a braided material to the hook and then fray out the end to make the tail. Wrap the long end of the material forward to make the body.

To finish a Skipping Shrimp, wrap the head area with a grizzly hackle to make a wet-fly collar. The metal eyes will make the fly swim with the point up.

## BARRACUDA FLIES

Barracudas are underrated gamefish. They hit hard, run fast, look (and are) dangerous, and take a fast-moving fly well. They also attain respectable sizes. The current IGFA fly-rod record is 48 pounds on a 20-pound-test class tippet, and the all-tackle record is 85 pounds. Although barracudas will eat almost anything, and can presumably catch anything they chase, the favored flies are slender patterns that resemble needlefish. Although there are a number of ways to tie these, none of them requires many materials.

### Braided 'Cuda Flies

Braided 'cuda flies are actually plaited, but they are simple to tie. They can be tied in single or multiple colors. The basic idea is to produce a long, skinny fly that will resemble a fleeing needlefish racing across the surface.

The body of this type of fly consists of three strands of material attached at the rear of the hook shank and then plaited. Wrapping the hook shank with the tying thread produces the head and long nose of the needlefish. A coat of epoxy on the thread-wrapped shank keeps a striking or hooked 'cuda from cutting the thread and ruining the fly. Sometimes eyes are added before the final epoxy coat.

**Hook:** Regular or long shank, stainless steel, size 3/0 through 2.
**Thread:** To match or contrast with the body/tail of the fly. Red and orange are popular thread colors.
**Body/tail:** Braided material such as any of those by Gudebrod or Kreinik, or plastic braids from craft stores. The body and tail can be solid green, chartreuse, yellow, white, black, red, pink, orange, or light blue; a two-tone color scheme such as red/white, black/white, yellow/green, pink/red, or blue/green; or three colors such as red/white/green, red/white/blue, red/pink/white, green/blue/lavender, or whatever else you can dream up. If you use two colors, one will dominate the other; in a pink/red body, for instance, two of the strands will be either pink or red.
**Head:** Thread neatly wrapped around the hook shank and tapered thin in the front.
**Eyes** (optional): Prism, doll, or 3-D plastic eyes, glued at the junction of the body/tail and head wrap.
**Finish:** Five-minute epoxy, to protect the thread from the teeth of a 'cuda.

This is a three-part tie. First, tie on the three body/tail materials, and wrap the thread evenly to the front of the hook, where you can tie it off. Second, secure the head of the fly and plait the three strands of braided material until you have made a body of the desired length. Secure the tail end of the plaited body by wrapping a band of thread around all three strands of material; tie off the band of thread with a whip finish. Third, glue on the eyes (these are optional) and then epoxy the entire head before placing the fly on a rotator to allow the epoxy to cure without sagging or dripping.

The easiest way to make these is with an assembly-line method. Tie on the body materials and make the thread wrap that will become the head. Then, with a number of these made, secure a fly to plait the tail. To do this, rig a small peg or brad nailed into the edge of your bench, onto which you can hang the eye of the hook. Then, with the tail materi-

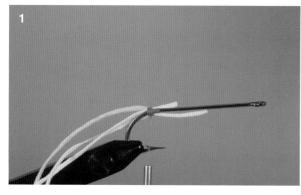

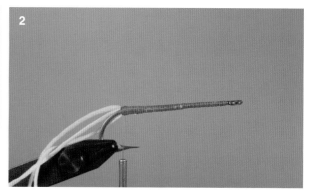

A Braided 'Cuda Fly uses three pieces of braided material for the tail. Attach the three strands to the rear of the hook shank.

Wrap the red thread forward and back to make the fly's long nose. Whip-finish the thread and clip it.

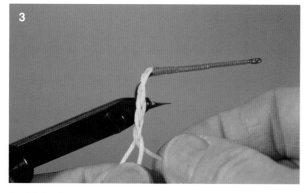

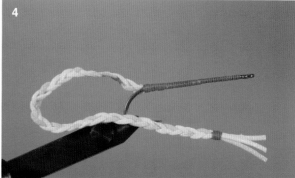

Braid the three pieces of material (technically, you're plaiting them). The piece on the left goes over the middle piece and under the right piece. Then, reverse to go right to left, following the same pattern.

Once you've plaited the tail to the desired length, secure the materials with a short band of thread. Tie off the band with a whip finish.

Glue eyes to the rear of the head. Coat the head and nose with epoxy to complete the Braided 'Cuda Fly.

als pointed toward you, plait them. An alternative is to turn the vise 90 degrees so that you can plait the tail.

Once at the end of the tail, remove the fly from the brad (or vise) and hold the end of the tail while beginning a wrap with tying thread. Wrap the thread around all three materials, clip the excess tag end of thread, and then complete the band with a whip finish. Use thread that matches the tail color, or use red or bright pink as a "triggering" point on the fly.

Plait all the flies you have prepared. Coat the tail wraps with a flexible, clear sealer such as Flexament or Softex. Stick or glue the eyes at the rear of each fly's head. Mix a batch of five-minute epoxy and coat the eyes and heads, using a disposable brush or bodkin. Place the flies on a low-rpm rotator to cure.

These are fished by making a long cast in front of the 'cuda and then retrieving with both hands, with the rod tucked between your knees or under one arm, to make the fly move fast. Don't worry about a 'cuda not being able to catch a fly that it wants.

### Twisted 'Cuda Fly

This is a simpler fly made with a single, twisted piece of material. The body is made like that of the Simple Bass Worm in chapter 6—a long piece of material attached to the hook, twisted, and then doubled back and allowed to furl itself into a rope or double helix. It has the advantage of not requiring plaiting or wrapping the tail. The main disadvantage of this fly is that not all body materials work well. The best products are yarns, macramé twist materials, and so forth. Some of the standard fly-tying body materials do not work well or require a precise number of turns to twist properly and look right in the water.

**Hook:** Regular or long shank, stainless steel, size 3/0 through 2.
**Thread:** To match the head color.
**Body/tail:** A single strand of macramé material or hard yarn (as opposed to soft, fuzzy yarn). White, yellow, black, green, blue, pink, red, and chartreuse are good colors.
**Head:** The same material as the body/tail, unless you're tying a variation (see below).
**Eyes:** Prism, plastic, or doll eyes.
**Finish:** Epoxy.

This style is tied by twisting the body/tail material to make it furl into a double helix and then wrapping the remaining material around the hook shank. You will need to start with a piece of material about three times the length of the intended body/tail. On most flies, the body/tail will be about 4 to 7 inches long, depending upon personal preference and what you feel you can cast. Therefore, you will start with a piece of material 12 to more than 20 inches long.

Attach the thread to the rear of the hook shank, and then secure one end of the body/tail material. Hold the material about two-thirds of its length from the hook and twist it. Do this in the direction of the manufacturer's twist so that you tighten the material rather than loosen it. After a few turns (experimentation will determine the best number of twists for each material and length), fold the twisted material over a bodkin and back to the hook shank. When you remove the bodkin, the material will furl or twist around itself to make

Begin a Twisted 'Cuda Fly by tying in one end of a long piece of braid material at the rear of the hook. Twist the material, and then fold it back on itsel. The material will furl itself into a two-strand rope like this. Tie the other end of the material to the hook.

Wrap the remaining material up the hook shank to make the fly's head and nose. Tie off the braid. Add eyes, and coat the head and nose with epoxy.

something that looks like a rope. Tie down the end of the material that you doubled back to the hook shank. You now have a rope extending from the rear of the hook, and a few inches of untwisted material pointing forward from the tie-down wraps.

Lift the untwisted material out of the way and wind the thread to the hook eye. Make the fly's head by wrapping the untwisted material up the hook shank. If you estimated the length correctly (this might also require a little experimentation), you will have just enough yarn to reach the hook eye. Secure the material, trim the excess, and whip-finish the thread. This method produces a thicker head than one made of thread alone, though you can adjust the head's thickness. To make a thicker head, twist the yarn a little before wrapping it, and make each wrap tight against the preceding one. For a thinner head, untwist the material to flatten it, and let the wraps barely touch one another. Glue the eyes (if you want them) at the rear of the hook shank, and then coat the head and eyes with five-minute epoxy. Place the fly on a rotator.

A variation is to furl the body, but then cut away all the leftover yarn and make the head with thread alone. This produces a very thin head like that of the Braided 'Cuda Fly. A thread head also lets you pick a color that will match or contrast with the tail material. Fish this style as you would any 'cuda fly—cast in front of the fish so as to not scare it, and retrieve very rapidly.

### Stranded 'Cuda Fly

Modern synthetic hairs let us use conventional tying methods to make 'cuda flies that are as long and as thin as we want. The best synthetic hairs for 'cuda flies are the heavier and tougher materials that can survive more than a single encounter with a barracuda's teeth. The individual fibers of materials such as Super Hair, FisHair, and the like are thicker and sturdier than the fine fibers of such materials as Aqua Fiber, Neer Hair, and similar products.

The Stranded 'Cuda Fly is a one-material pattern. It's easy to tie, though it does require a band of thread at the tail end (as does the Braided 'Cuda Fly). Like our other barracuda flies, this one has a coat of epoxy on the head.

**Hook:** Regular or long shank, stainless steel, size 3/0 through 2.

**Thread:** To match or contrast with the body/tail color.

**Body/tail:** A 4- to 7-inch bundle of Super Hair or similar material. White, black, green, yellow, chartreuse, light blue, light green, lavender, orange, and pink are all good colors.

**Head:** The tying thread, wrapped on the hook shank to make a long nose.

**Eyes:** Prism, doll, or plastic eyes attached at the rear of the head.

**Finish:** Epoxy over the head and eyes.

To make a sturdy fly, first attach the thread at the rear of the hook shank, and then tie in the bundle of synthetic hair. Make sure that the butts are long enough to extend the full length of the hook shank. This helps secure the material to the hook and makes for a more durable fly. Taper the butts by trimming them with coarse scissors; this will give the head a corresponding taper. Then wrap the thread forward over the butts. You can wrap a single layer of thread, making each turn lie against the the previous one, or you can spiral-wrap the thread to secure the butts of the synthetic hair and then wrap back and forth to completely cover the head area with thread. No matter how you do it, try to produce a neat, smooth head. Whip-finish the thread, glue the eyes in place, and coat the head and eyes with epoxy. After the epoxy cures, wrap a band of thread around the fibers at the tail of the fly. Seal the tail wrap with Softex or Flexament. Or you can wrap the tail first and then epoxy the head and eyes.

An obvious variation is to use two or more colors of synthetic hair to make a fly with a darker back. Besides increasing the fly's complexity, each additional clump of hair can increase the fly's bulk if you're not careful. A two- or three-color 'cuda fly should be no thicker than a single-color fly.

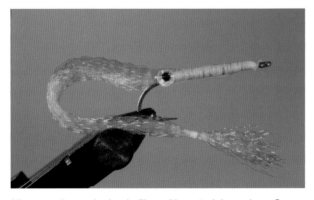

You can also make 'cuda flies with materials such as Super Hair. Tie a long, thin clump of synthetic hair to the hook. Wrap the shank with a braid to make the head. Make a short band of thread at the tail end of the Super Hair. Add eyes, and give the head a coat of epoxy. Seal the tail wrap with Softex or Flexament.

### Plaited-Strand 'Cuda Fly

This fly also consists of a bundle of synthetic hair, but the hair is divided into three approximately equal sections that are then plaited. The overall effect is a cross between the Braided 'Cuda Fly and the Stranded 'Cuda Fly.

**Hook:** Regular or long shank, stainless steel, size 3/0 through 2.
**Thread:** To match or contrast with the body/tail.
**Body/tail:** A bundle of synthetic hair divided into three smaller clumps and plaited. Effective colors include white, black, red, pink, yellow, chartreuse, green, blue, orange, and lavender.
**Head:** The tying thread, wrapped on the hook shank to make a long nose.
**Eyes:** Prism, doll, or plastic eyes attached at the rear of the head.
**Finish:** Epoxy over the head and eyes.

Plaiting the synthetic hair makes for a fly with a tighter body, a little more durability, and less chance of individual fibers creeping out. After attaching the thread to the hook, secure the bundle of synthetic hair. Taper the butts and make the thread-wrapped head. Hook the fly onto a peg or turn the vise 90 degrees, and divide the plastic hair into three bundles. Plait the bundles to make the fly's body. Secure the tail end of the plaited body with a band of thread. Seal the tail wrap with Softex, Flexament, or a similarly flexible sealer. Add the eyes and coat the head with epoxy.

A clump of Super Hair or a similar material can be divided into three parts and plaited to make a long, thin body. Plastic eyes and epoxy complete the fly.

Examples of 'cuda flies. Top to bottom: plaited, twisted, stranded, and plaited-stranded.

## TARPON FLIES

Many tarpon flies fall into two broad categories: light, slender designs for sight-casting in shallow water; and bushy, heavier styles such as Whistlers for fishing in deep water, strong currents, or dirty water where the angler needs a fly that "pushes water." Flies of the latter type are also useful for general saltwater fly fishing (see chapter 9). Let's concentrate on the light, slender style of tarpon fly. One simple design can serve as the model for many patterns.

### Easy Apte Tarpon Fly

Writer, tackle consultant, and former tarpon guide Stu Apte is credited as the first to develop this slim, tapered, Keys-style tarpon fly designed for clear, shallow water. It is tied much like a Seaducer, but a little sparser and with the collar restricted to the rear of the hook. Although developed for tarpon, this basic design can be used for many other saltwater gamefish.

To tie a simple Stu Apte-style tarpon fly, begin by tying in the tail of splayed saddle hackles. Then attach a saddle hackle to be wrapped in front of the tail.

Wrap the collar hackle just in front of the tail. If the collar doesn't want to slope to the rear, use a few wraps of thread to force the fibers to lie rearward.

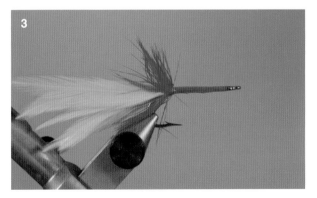

Complete the fly by wrapping the red thread forward and then back. After whip-finishing, seal all the exposed thread with epoxy or colored enamel.

**Hook:** Regular-length stainless-steel or saltwater hook, size 4/0 through 2.
**Thread:** Usually red, but you can use other colors to match or contrast with the feathers.
**Tail/wing:** Saddle or neck hackles. Good colors range from bright shades (white, yellow, orange, pink, and red) to black, blue, and various colors of dyed grizzly.
**Collar:** Hackle matching or contrasting with the tail/wing. Wrapped at the rear of the hook shank, the collar lies back at an angle.

Attach the thread at the rear of the hook shank. Tie the tail/wing feathers as far back on the shank as you can so that they won't foul when you cast the fly. The tails are usually splayed outward. Attach and wrap a hackle at the rear of the hook shank. Unlike the collar of a Seaducer, this fly's hackle covers only the rearmost portion of the shank. To finish the fly, make a long, even wrap of thread up and then back down the hook shank. Tie off the thread. Seal the exposed thread with epoxy or a coat of red, orange, or similarly bright lacquer or enamel.

# chapter

# 11

Historical and current information provides ample evidence of the effectiveness of simple flies. Dry-fly gurus Halford and Marryat chanced upon simplicity more than 100 years ago by accidentally tying dry flies without bodies that proved just as effective as the standard, fully dressed models. Lefty Kreh proved that simple is good with his bottle-cork Potomac River Popper. The one-material Glo Bug has become a standard for trout, Pacific salmon, and steelhead. Two-material Bivisibles are classic trout drys. Two-or three-material soft-hackle wet flies are increasing in popularity. Simple streamers of only a few parts dominate much inshore saltwater fishing.

The point is that although complexity of pattern and exactness of imitation are marvelous to look at and proof of fly-tying skill, they are not the gauge of effectiveness. Often the fly with a few parts and soft materials such as rabbit fur or marabou will look better in the water and provoke more strikes than a fly that looks like a twin of a natural.

Remember that nearly any pattern book will provide dozens to hundreds of patterns that would fill the three-materials-or-fewer requirement of this book. The concept of simple flies is not new or foreign to the art of fly tying. It seems new when you try to convince tiers that they might not need a body or wings on a dry fly, that they can veil a streamer's wing around a hook and eliminate the pattern's body, that they can make simple nymphs of three materials that will suggest all the necessary parts (thorax, abdomen, wing case, legs, gills) that persuade a trout to hit the fly.

Remember also that how flies are *fished* makes all the difference. Whether you cast a multi-material, complex design or a two-material, two-minute fly, you still have to know where to cast it and how to fish the fly so that it represents whatever kind of fish food it was designed to imitate. Results depend on the angler.

### CREATING SIMPLE FLIES

In business and other circles of society, developing new concepts, products, philosophies, and so forth is often called "thinking outside the box." That has always struck me as a strange image, but the implication is that you have to think in ways other than the standard, established, "approved" methods. The same applies to fly tying, and the best and brightest fly tiers think this way all the time. Tying simple flies, and particularly originating them, requires thinking outside the box. You need imagination to find new ways to use old materials or ways to employ materials not designed for fly tying to help you make a better, more effective, and simpler fly.

In part, this might involve thinking about existing fly-tying materials and considering new ways to use them. Can you use a strange-looking yarn as a hackle? Can Thin Skin be wrapped as a body? Will ostrich work as a streamer wing? I am not sure that any of these thoughts will work very well. But the ideas of using rabbit-skin strips for Zonkers, wrapping marabou on hooks to make fuzzy nymphs, employing beads as nymph heads, bending hooks to make upside-down flies, paring down a beetle imitation to a coffee bean and a few fibers, coating the heads or bodies of flies with epoxy, and tying flies with plastic materials all came from people thinking in ways not found in the books or standard patterns of the time.

The idea behind simple flies is not to slavishly follow a "three-materials-or-fewer" rule, but to follow your own thoughts to the simplest way to make the best fly that will catch fish. One material? Two materials? Three? Four? More than four materials? I tie and use them all. The bottom line is to stock the fly box and try the contents on the water. Have fun—and keep it simple.

# BIBLIOGRAPHY

Best, A. K. *Production Fly Tying*. Boulder, CO: Pruett Publishing Co., 1989.

Bruce, Joe. *Fly Design Theory and Practice*. Lisbon, MD: K & D Publishing, 2002.

Fullum, Jay "Fishy." *Fishy's Flies*. Mechanicsburg, PA: Stackpole Books, 2002.

Kreh, Lefty. *Saltwater Fly Patterns*. New York: Lyons & Burford, 1995.

Leeson, Ted and Jim Schollmeyer. *The Fly Tier's Benchside Reference*. Portland, OR: Frank Amato Publications, 1998.

Likakis, John. *Bass Bug Basics*. Woodstock, VT: The Countryman Press, 2003.

Martin, Darrel. *Fly-Tying Methods*. New York: Nick Lyons Books, 1987.

Meck, Charles. *101 Innovative Fly-Tying Tips*. Guilford, CT: The Lyons Press, 2002.

Moore, Wayne. *Fly Tying Notes*. Seattle, WA: Recreational Consultants, 1984.

Morris, Skip. *Tying Foam Flies*. Portland, OR: Frank Amato Publications, 1994.

Pfeiffer, C. Boyd. *Bug Making*. New York: Lyons and Burford, 1993.

Pfeiffer, C. Boyd. *Fly Fishing Bass Basics*. Mechanicsburg, PA: Stackpole Books, 1997.

Pfeiffer, C. Boyd. *Fly Fishing Saltwater Basics*. Mechanicsburg, PA: Stackpole Books, 1999.

Pfeiffer, C. Boyd. *Shad Fishing*. Mechanicsburg, PA: Stackpole Books, 2002.

Pfeiffer, C. Boyd. *The Complete Photo Guide to Fly Tying Tips*. Chanhassen, MN: Creative Publishing Int., 2005.

Pfeiffer, C. Boyd. *Tying Trout Flies*. Iola, WI: Krause Publications, 2002.

Pfeiffer, C. Boyd. *Tying Warmwater Flies*. Iola, WI: Krause Publications, 2003.

Scheck, Art. *Tying Better Flies*. Woodstock, VT: The Countryman Press, 2003.

Schollmeyer, Jim and Ted Leeson. *Tying Emergers*. Portland, OR: Frank Amato Publications, 2004.

Steeves, Harrison R. III. *Tying Flies with Foam, Fur, and Feathers*. Mechanicsburg, PA: Stackpole Books, 2003.

Stewart, Dick. *Fly-Tying Tips*. Intervale, NH: Northland Press Inc., 1990.

Talleur, Richard W. *The Fly Tyer's Primer*. New York: Winchester Press, 1986.

Talleur, Dick. *The Versatile Fly Tyer*. New York: Nick Lyons Books, 1990.

Tryon, Chuck and Sharon. *Figuring Out Flies*. Rolla, MO: Ozark Mountain Fly Fishers, 1990.

Veniard, John and Donald Downs. *Fly-Tying Problems and Their Answers*. New York: Crown Publishers, 1972.

Warren, Joe J. *Tying Glass Bead Flies.* Portland, OR: Frank Amato Publications, 1997.

Williamson, Robert. *Creative Flies: Innovative Tying Techniques.* Portland, OR: Frank Amato Publications, 2002.

# INDEX

# INDEX